Historic Halifax

Plate 1. Red Chamber, Province House

Historic Halifax

Photographs by Alvin Comiter

Text by Elizabeth Pacey

HOUNSLOW

For my mother and father, Aunt Tannie, and Aunt Becky
- Alvin Comiter

For my husband Philip, my mother Mildred Young,
and to the memory of my father John Young
- Elizabeth Pacey

Historic Halifax

Text Copyright © 1988 Elizabeth Pacey
Photographs Copyright © 1988 Alvin Comiter

All Rights Reserved

ISBN 0-88882-103-4

Publisher: Anthony Hawke
Design: Next Step Graphics
Composition: Braemar Publishers
Printer: Friesen Printers

Hounslow Press
A Division of Anthony R. Hawke Limited
124 Parkview Avenue
Willowdale, Ontario
Canada   M2N 3Y5

Publication was assisted by the Canada Council
and the Ontario Arts Council.

Printed and bound in Canada

O ur purpose in preparing *Historic Halifax* was to celebrate, in photographs and words, the registered heritage properties of Halifax. We hope that the selected buildings and streetscapes indicate the remarkable range of architectural styles still extant in Halifax. The descriptions highlight historical personages or events associated with the buildings.

A number of buildings that are not yet registered have been included because of their significance to the city's historic fabric. Their presence in the book also points out the ongoing nature of the registration process. Though the number of registered buildings, about 290, may seem substantial, it is relatively small for such an historic city. A great deal has been done, but there is more to do.

The organization of the material corresponds generally to the geography of the city. For example, the Old Town within the palisades was roughly bounded by Citadel Hill, the waterfront, Cogswell Street and Spring Garden Road; in that section we also have included the Public Gardens and Summer Street west of Citadel Hill. The South Suburbs section encompasses the earliest suburbs immediately south of Spring Garden Road and historic buildings as far south as Point Pleasant Park and as far west as Oxford Street. Similarly, the North Suburbs section extends past the oldest northern suburbs to the Prince's Lodge Rotunda, the most northerly historic building within the present city limits. We hope this arrangement will provide an armchair tour from the southern tip to the northern boundary of Halifax.

The authors have many people to thank. For valuable discussions we are indebted to Shirley Elliott, Jill Grant, Lyndon Watkins and Jean Weir. For research assistance, we are especially grateful to the staffs of the Reference Department of the Halifax City Regional Library, the Legislative Library, and the Public Archives of Nova Scotia, Garry Shutlak,

Harold Pearse, Donald Soucy, Gerald Vickers, and Maud Rosinski .

We offer special thanks to Chris Nielsen who provided expert darkroom assistance. Several individuals arranged interior photography sessions including Pam Veinotte and John Grenville (Halifax Citadel), Joyce and Paul McCulloch (Bollard House), Rev. Ivan Norton (Fort Massey Church), Rev. Edward Thompson (St. Matthew's Church), Rev. Robert Petit (St. George's Church), the Nova Scotia Barristers Society (Keith Hall) and George Somers (Prince's Lodge Rotunda). We would also like to thank the Canada Council Explorations Program and the Nova Scotia College of Art and Design for grants to purchase photographic materials.

We are particularly pleased with the cooperation of the City of Halifax. From the outset, Mayor Ron Wallace and members of City Council have expressed a keen interest in the book. The members of the Heritage Advisory Committee, Commodore A. C. McMillin (Chair), Joan Malay (Vice-Chair), Barbara Watt (Chair of the Public Relations Sub-Committee), Dr. L. W. Collins, Dan Goodspeed, Alderman D. Grant, Alderman A. Hamshaw, Mary O. Hebb, A. Bernard Inglis, Tim Margolian, Ian McDermaid, Alderman N. Meagher, George Rogers and Susan Torrens have not only shepherded the historic buildings through the registration process but have enthusiastically endorsed this project. For their very considerable efforts on behalf of the city, we applaud them. A. W. Churchill, Rita Fraser and Deborah Chambers of city staff offered valuable advice and technical assistance.

We sincerely hope this book will foster a greater awareness of the rich built heritage of historic Halifax.

Alvin Comiter
Elizabeth Pacey   June, 1988

*H*istoric Halifax by Elizabeth Pacey and Alvin Comiter is a crisp, clear record of our heritage. They have "stopped in time" one hundred heritage buildings and streetscapes that encompass a time span of two and one-half centuries. This is how they looked in 1988.

Here we have a valuable family album assembled for the record. These are the heroic survivors. They are all standing monuments to the wars, the depression, the explosion, and the passing years. Above all, they have character. They remain members of the Halifax family, bonded by time and affection, and shared experiences. They belong.

An informed public is the best defence against erosion of our heritage. This book adds a new defence and an additional inventory of our existing resources. Taking stock now helps us plan for the future. These are not dormant artifacts or museums, but a living, evolving, exciting part of the fabric of the City. Pierre Berton said "heritage is a marketable commodity". Historic Properties and so many of our heritage buildings have taken on a new role in our life, changing focus, function and direction.

In *Historic Halifax*, we pause to celebrate the worthy survivors from the past that add so much to our City as they travel with us into the future.

May those who plan our future have the imagination and courage to respect our past.

"THE PAST IS PROLOGUE"

Ron Wallace
MAYOR

Founded in 1749 as the British stronghold on the western North Atlantic, Halifax had a definite identity even as a raw garrison town behind the rough-hewn piquets of the palisade. Through the vicissitudes of more than two centuries, the little town on the great harbour became steadily more distinctive. From the enterprising years of sailing ships and privateers to the bustling years of the Second World War when convoys congregated in the harbour, Halifax grew in character.

By the middle of the 20th century, Halifax had settled into its role as Canada's most historic English-speaking city. But like family wealth inherited by successive generations, the city's rich historical endowment was taken for granted.

It was not till the 1960's that the historic fabric of downtown Halifax began to change radically. Both the Bank of Montreal and the Royal Bank sacrificed architecturally significant buildings for high-rise towers. An 18-block site containing several important historic structures was cleared and the nine towers of Scotia Square began to rise above the rubble.

Finally, when a proposed expressway threatened to mow down seven antiquated waterfront warehouses, public opinion galvanized to stop the annihilation. The archetypal struggle to save those tangible representatives of the city's glorious sea-faring past marked an important turning point. Never again could the existence of the city's historic buildings be taken for granted.

The victory on the waterfront was followed by both euphoria and disillusionment. Euphoria because the warehouses had been rescued and recognized as a National Historic Site, yet disillusionment because similar success with other valuable historic structures was not easy to repeat. General public opinion and a protest march by outraged architecture students could not save the magnificent old Doull and Miller Building on the south-west corner of Prince and Hollis streets. Two more banks, the Toronto Dominion and the Imperial Bank of Commerce, together laid waste to almost an entire block of early buildings. And towers replaced the Capitol Theatre that fell dramatically, its grand red velvet curtain billowing with each grotesque swing of the wrecking ball.

Part of the reason for such losses after the major victory was ownership. The waterfront buildings were city-owned and Halifax City Council was accountable to the citizens for its decisions regarding public land. The other properties were owned by commercial companies. Company profits took precedence over public wishes in those cases. City Council was powerless to prevent demolition of any privately-owned building, historic or not.

It was sobering to realize that the distinctive face of Halifax might be completely unrecognizable in a few

Plate 2.   Old Town Clock, Citadel Hill

short years. Especially since the downtown core had, seemingly overnight, become the prime commercial real estate in the Maritimes.

It was even more sobering to realize that City Council could not readily be given the power to control demolition. Cities are the creatures of the provinces, and there was no provincial enabling legislation on the books. All of the other nine provinces had heritage legislation but historic Nova Scotia did not!

Through the mid-1970's, preservationists lobbied for protective legislation. And the wheels of the provincial government began to turn. As "green and white" papers were spewed forth for public comment, the city's planning staff prepared for the eventual passage of the legislation. Criteria were developed for judging the historic and architectural significance of buildings. With the aid of volunteer heritage enthusiasts who spent six months researching more than one hundred specific buildings, a preliminary group of historic buildings was selected. Information on each of these successful candidates and on the scoring system was published in the 1977 report, *An Evaluation and Protection System for Heritage Resources in Halifax.*

Three more years elapsed before the provincial Heritage Property Act was at last proclaimed in 1980. Under the new Act, a two-tier preservation system was established. Buildings or sites registered by the provincial government could not be demolished. Buildings registered by a municipality, on the other hand, were not so well protected; provision was made for a one-year delay before the demolition or significant alteration of a registered property could take place. Legislators reasoned that owners might oppose widespread registration of heritage properties at the municipal level if an absolute ban on demolition or major alteration were enacted.

The capital city played a leading role in implementing the Heritage Property Act. Not only had some of the ground work been done on researching and scoring a preliminary list of buildings, but elected representatives moved swiftly to constitute the Heritage Advisory Committee which would formally recommend heritage properties to City Council for registration. The process, involving evaluations, reports and hearings for the owners, got under way. To date, approximately 290 heritage properties, including individual buildings, sites and streetscapes, have been registered. The vast majority of owners willingly accepted the special status of their buildings. Some owners have even applied for registration.

In spite of relatively smooth beginnings, the situation, now eight years after the the passage of the Act, is not entirely positive. Like an automobile that is subjected to long-term road-testing for the first time, bugs have begun to appear in the system. For example, a number of meritorious properties have not been registered because of the owners' objections; sadly, some of those properties were bulldozed abruptly with no leeway to find other alternatives.

An even more serious problem, certainly unforeseen by those who drafted the Act, occurs when developers acquire registered historic buildings with the sole intention of tearing them down. In the face of such actions, governments must consider purchasing the threatened heritage properties with a view to re-selling them to more tractable owners.

There is no room for tepidity or timidity. For the demolition-delay mechanism of the Heritage Property Act to be workable, as it has proved to be in other jurisdictions, the political will must continue to be strong. If the will is weak, Halifax will soon have little left to show for its illustrious past; it will be a city robbed of its roots. But if the will stands firm, Halifax can march with dignity into the next century, still in the forefront of the nation's heritage □

SOUTH SUBURBS

On June 21, 1749, Colonel Edward Cornwallis sailed into the deep-water harbour aboard the Sloop of War *Sphinx* to found the garrison town of Halifax. At first he chose the tip of the peninsula as the site for the new settlement. The fleet of 13 transports arrived with 2576 settlers who were soon employed cutting down trees. But the point of land was far too exposed to the strong blasts of the prevailing winds and a more sheltered situation was soon chosen two miles further up the harbour.

However, the strategic location of Point Pleasant ensured its use in the network of harbour defences. In 1762, shortly after St. John's, Newfoundland, was captured by the French in a surprise attack, two gun batteries were set up on either side of the point to guard the harbour approaches and the entrance to the Northwest Arm. In 1793, at the onset of the Revolutionary War with France, Brigadier-General James Ogilvie added Fort Ogilvie, a crescent-shaped earthen battery, on the harbour side of the point. The strength of the seaside batteries was further bolstered by the construction of the Prince of Wales Tower on high ground. And lastly, in 1862, the threat of American invasion during the American Civil War prompted the building of a fourth battery with 12 powerful rifled muzzle loaders.

In spite of 100 years of preparation, no attack came. And the 186 acres of unspoiled, natural landscape with spectacular vistas of the broad harbour and the narrow Northwest Arm were coveted for a park.

Thus, in 1866, the Crown leased Point Pleasant to a nine-member Board of Commissioners for 999 years at a yearly rent of one shilling.

In 1896 an official residence for the Park Keeper was constructed at the northern edge of the park. The rough-faced stone house with steeply stepped Gothic gables adds to the scenic context against the wooded backdrop of the park.

For more than a century citizens have benefitted from the efforts of the Park Keeper and the public-spirited Commissioners. Point Pleasant Park lives up to its name admirably. Nothing is more 'pleasant' for body and soul than a brisk walk along the forested paths where scents of fir and spruce mingle with salt sea air, and great black-backed gulls wheel high above □

Plate 3.   Point Pleasant Lodge, Point Pleasant Park

*I*lluminated by light from the gun porthole, the cavernous interior with its thick vaulted ceiling recalls the days when 6-pounder guns stood guard at the portholes, and the heavy armament on the gun platform above was ready for a military emergency. In response to just such an emergency, the tower had been built by a young prince who broke the rules, and his engineer who was an innovator of military strategy.

In the spring of 1796, fear of attack swept over Halifax; a French squadron had arrived at Santo Domingo and could very easily travel up the coast of North America and bombard the British outposts. Captain James Straton, the Commanding Royal Engineer, recommended the construction of a stone coastal defence tower on Point Pleasant.

Prince Edward, fourth son of King George III and Commander-in-Chief of the garrison, forged ahead without proper government approval. When the tower was two-thirds finished, the prince was officially rebuked for breaking the King's regulations which prohibited the ad hoc construction of permanent forts. As a consequence, the incomplete project was halted.

However, Prince Edward's persuasive arguments finally won support in Britain and construction of the tower continued to completion. Named for Edward's favourite brother, George, Prince of Wales, the tower stands as the first martello tower in the British Empire and the forerunner of 136 more that were built in the British Isles and Canada □

Plate 4. Prince of Wales Tower, Point Pleasant Park

anada's National Council of Women, founded in 1893 by the Countess of Aberdeen, was devoted to the advancement of women and the betterment of health care and social conditions. The Halifax Chapter, founded a year later, was lauded by the *Winnipeg Chronicle* as an "organization which has bound together all individual workers as well as similar bands of organized workers into a great harmonious whole". Indeed the group has been instrumental in setting up the Victorian Order of Nurses, hostels for immigrants, and supervised playgrounds. They have fought for such diverse causes as cleanliness at the slaughterhouse and the vote for women.

In 1903, this residence was built for businessman George Wright. The dramatic design with the pillared portico, tall, conical-capped tower and half-timber Tudor touches, was the work of J. C. Dumaresq.

Wright travelled widely, not just on business ventures but on personal missions to help stamp out the evils of society. He toured towns and cities alike, lecturing on intemperance, profanity and immorality. In the spring of 1912, while on a trip to London, England, he wisely wrote his will, philanthropically dispersing his $226,000 estate to churches, charities and worthy causes. Though he had been a confirmed bachelor, he left his splendid residence to the Council of Women "to be used as an institution for carrying on their work and assist in suppressing other evils such as I have been writing about and trying to put down".

The house might not have passed so quickly to the Women's Council if George Wright had not been such a wealthy and frequent traveller. But alas, he booked his return passage from England on the maiden voyage of the reputedly unsinkable luxury liner *Titanic*!

Plate 5.   Women's Council House, 989 Young Avenue

*B*ehind the protective wrought-iron railing the gracious Georgian home reposes. Its exact date of construction was discovered when a hand-written builder's note, dated August 1, 1834, was found on the old wallboards of the original basement kitchen; the note listed the first names of the workmen and the tasks they were to carry out. In the spring of 1838, the house was advertised for sale "with nine finished rooms, excellent kitchen and frost proof cellar". One of the surprising indoor "conveniences" of the kitchen was an open well in the centre of the floor. Such modern amenities and the stylish design of the house accounted for its quick sale to James Forman for £1,110.

James Forman, along with other prominent citizens, had successfully petitioned the House of Assembly for the incorporation of the Bank of Nova Scotia in 1832. Forman had then been appointed chief cashier, a position of great trust akin to that of general manager today. Though a few new branches opened during Forman's more than 30-year tenure, the Bank's monetary assets showed only meager gains. One reason for the slow growth was brought to light by an accountant in 1870; during his career, Forman had embezzled approximately half the Bank's capital — a sum of $314,967.68!

James Forman was never prosecuted. Perhaps his "untouchable" social position saved him from the ignominy, or perhaps the public was sympathetic to his failing health and the rumour that he had taken

the money to alleviate his son's financial troubles. In partial restitution, Forman transferred properties worth $179,296.45 to the Bank. He then departed hastily for London where he died shortly afterwards.

Whether the ghost of James Forman still lingers at Thorndean is disputable. But one night during restorations to the house, a workman was awakened by the persistent nudging of a ghostly presence who then beckoned the sleepy workman towards the indoor well in the old kitchen. The workman was frightened of being pushed in, and absconded from the job at daybreak. But maybe the ghostly message was only one of buried treasure!

Plate 6. Thorndean, 5680 Inglis Street

*T*he January 4, 1896, edition of the *Halifax Herald* proudly announced that more than 120 buildings, valued at $500,550, had been constructed in the city in 1895. The increased variety in the styles of the residences was noted, with special reference to the fashionable "Gable roofs and Queen Anne cottages". The "magnificent residence" of Mr. Harshaw B. Clarke was praised as "one of the most ornamental and expansive houses in Halifax". Constructed at a cost of $17,000, and designed by the architectural firm of Elliot and Hopson, the house represents the Queen Anne style on a grand scale. A proliferation of gable-roofed bay windows, verandas and a domed corner turret surprise the beholder. Harshaw Clarke, then manager of the Academy of Music, stayed only six years. In 1905, prominent corporation lawyer, Robert E. Harris, and his wife Minnie purchased the house.

Born in Annapolis Royal, Harris had reached the top of his profession by his "indomitable zeal" and a genius for diplomatically solving company problems. He succeeded at the 'sticky' task of amalgamating three maritime sugar refineries to form the new Acadia Sugar Refining Company, and he helped organize the Eastern Trust Company of which he was President for ten years. He also served as President of the Trinidad Electric Railway Company and the Nova Scotia Steel and Coal Company.

Harris gave up his large business income when he was appointed to the Supreme Court of Nova Scotia in 1915. So sound was his reasoning and so wise and clear were his decisions that he was quickly elevated to Chief Justice □

Plate 7. Clarke-Harris House, 1029 South Park Street

Fort Massey United Church stands on the site of the old Fort Massey, a blockhouse that formed part of the early defence network around Halifax. But the establishment of the church did not emerge from any link with its warlike antecedent but from the sweetest and most docile of sources — a happy children's group! In 1868, Fort Massey District Sunday School was opened in the expanding southern suburb by two other established churches. The school's success prompted the building of the new mother church.

In order to ensure an excellent architectural design a competition was held. Scottish-born architect, David Stirling, whose designs for the Halifax Club and St. David's Church were already highly regarded, was the winner. On June 25, 1870, the cornerstone was laid. The expensive project was carried out by Brookfield and Company for approximately $42,000. John Sheriff was the sculptor for superb Gothic embellishments such as the magnificent triple-arched portal carved in red sandstone.

When Fort Massey opened in 1871, an enthusiastic account in the *Halifax Reporter* noted, "the interior has a rich and pleasing effect and with a multitude of pillars, corbels and arches has almost a cathedral appearance". Certainly the remarkable variety of Gothic windows with more than 25 variations of intricate tracery can best be appreciated from the inside. The richly-carved wooden ceiling braces and hammer-beams as well as ornamental foliage,

kings' heads and trefoil arches in plasterwork all add to the Gothic opulence. Perched at intervals along the clerestory, medieval winged gorgons peer down upon the nave, protecting modern churchgoers from evil spirits!

The perfection of such details pleased a reporter for the *Canadian Illustrated News* in 1873 when the church was praised as "one of the most handsome specimens of Gothic architecture to be met in the Dominion" □

Plate 8. *Interior detail, Fort Massey Church, 1181 Queen Street*

SCHMIDTVILLE
COTTAGES

1318-1320
Birmingham Street

1329-1333
Birmingham Street

1317 Dresden Row

1345 Dresden Row

*I*n 1781, James Pedley, a merchant who had come from Birmingham, England, twenty years earlier, purchased 12 acres of land from Richard Bulkeley, one of the founding fathers of Halifax. The land, valued at £300 and located west of Queen Street, became known as Pedley's Fields. By his will of 1807, James Pedley bequeathed Pedley's Fields to his married daughter, Elizabeth Schmidt, for her own "use and behoof" independent of her husband's control.

Pedley may not have been overly fond of his son-in-law, Christian Schmidt, but a contemporary account described Schmidt as "a brave and zealous officer and faithful to his king and country." Christian Schmidt was a native of Rottenburg, Germany, who became a captain in King George III's Royal Foreign Artillery. He served with the British Forces during the American Revolution of 1776, and then came to Halifax where he married Elizabeth Pedley. The couple had six children. The three daughters, Rosina, Margaretta and Mary Ann are believed to have lived in the earliest cottages on Pedley's Fields.

In 1830, Elizabeth Schmidt, then a widow, allowed Pedley's Field to be subdivided into small building lots. The new suburb became known as Schmidt Ville. Two streets, Dresden Row and Rottenburg (now Clyde), were named in honour of her husband's German ancestry, and one street, Birmingham, was named for her father's birthplace.

Schmidtville is a fascinating neighborhood with the old-world intimacy of narrow streets neatly lined with urban cottages. The earliest group of structures included the mirror-image cottages at 1318-1320 Birmingham which pre-date the subdivision of the area. An inkling of their extreme age was discovered recently when coins dating back to 1814 were found under the floorboards by the owner, Lyndon Watkins.

At 1329-1333 Birmingham, another pair of mirror-image cottages were probably built not long after subdivision when Scottish dormers were at the height of fashion. At 1317 Dresden Row, one cottage was constructed in the style of a miniature mansion with a classical, triangular pediment and decorative stepped trilight window. Further up the street, at 1345 Dresden Row, an unembellished rectangular box-like cottage, built after 1850, defies the Victorian ideal of ornate architecture!

Plate 9. 1318-1320 Birmingham Street

Plate 11. 1317 Dresden Row

Plate 10. 1329-1333 Birmingham Street

Plate 12. 1345 Dresden Row

The Boak House is an intriguing architectural hybrid. The "trompe l'oeil" facade offers many clues to the evolution of styles in Halifax. After "gentleman" Samuel Story purchased the land in 1825, a simple one-storey cottage of native fieldstone with a smooth sandstone front was constructed. Later, a larger Georgian townhouse was created with the addition of a second storey of predominantly timber construction; fieldstone was, however, used for the side of the house containing the chimney. The townhouse had a typical truncated pitched roof. Still later in the century, the house was Victorianized. The roof was raised and a "half-mansard" formed on the front. On the sandstone-faced lower storey, the windows were enlarged and trimmed with keystones. Above the sandstone, wide ship-lapped boards imitate stonework, and a moulded wooden belt course indicates the elevated Victorian ceiling inside.

Robert Boak had been apprenticed to John Esson's importing firm at the age of fifteen. He rose to become the sole owner of the large shipping business including two wharves, four warehouses and three vessels. He was staunchly opposed to Confederation and served as President of the Repeal League in 1869. In 1872, he was appointed to the Legislative Council and acted as Provincial Treasurer in 1877-78.

Robert Boak conveyed the house to his son George Esson Boak who operated a cod processing plant and traded in fish, coal and oil. George Boak's family continuously owned and occupied the house for close to a century.

Unlike the Boak House, the adjacent Cunard-Wilson House has remained virtually unchanged. Built about 1834 on the eastern part of Samuel Story's lot, the Georgian townhouse still retains its original truncated pitched roof and Scottish dormers. The pretty Ionic, scroll-topped pilasters framing the doorway probably appealed to Margaret Cunard when she purchased the house in 1863.

Margaret Cunard was the widow of Edward Cunard, a younger brother of Samuel Cunard, Nova Scotia's most famous shipping magnate and initiator of the transatlantic Cunard Steamship Line. Before the days of steam, Edward had been master of various Cunard sailing ships; by 1825 he ran the Halifax office of the firm and in 1840 he had five vessels registered in his own name. In partnership with another brother, Joseph, he conducted an aggressive lumber business on the banks of the Miramichi in New Brunswick.

Margaret Cunard occupied the townhouse with her daughter Emily and son George. Early in this century, the house became the childhood home of Mrs. Mary Rudderham Wilson who still resides there with her husband □

Plate 14. Cunard-Wilson House, 5270 Morris Street

Plate 13 . Boak House, 5274 Morris Street

Crofton Uniacke, second son of the influential Attorney General Richard John Uniacke, was born in 1783. After studying law abroad, he returned to Nova Scotia, married Dorothy Fawson, and in 1807 purchased a large tract of land on Morris Street. That same year, his dressed stone townhouse was constructed. Dorothy Uniacke was entrusted to oversee the finishing touches while Crofton travelled on horseback through the Annapolis Valley with the circuit court.

By letter, Crofton reported to his "dear Dolly" about a delicious breakfast of "Jonney Cakes" in Windsor, and issued precise instructions for her to obey: "Do not neglect to have everything ready at the house for our moving in on my return." The order was mollified by his insistence on paying all the bills for any household purchases of her choice.

Crofton Uniacke rose to be Judge of the Vice-Admiralty Court before leaving for London in 1816. There he served as a barrister at the prestigious Lincoln's Inn and was counsel at the trial of the adulterous Queen Charlotte, wife of King George IV. Foreshadowing a modern approach to the "double standard", he wrote open letters to the debauched King arguing that it was immoral to condemn a woman for sins that are overlooked when committed by men.

Before leaving Halifax, Crofton Uniacke had sold his house to Richard Harney, a neighbour and prosperous butcher. The unusual "sale" made provision for

Crofton's brother, Richard John Uniacke Junior, to occupy the premises, with the full price not due until five years later.

A magnificent fanlight and corner quoins decorate this Georgian townhouse. In keeping with late 19th century architectural fashions, a "half-mansard" roof with two ornamental dormers was added; a third central dormer was incorporated more recently. Built to endure for centuries, the Crofton Uniacke House is the only solid granite house in Halifax □

Plate 15.   Crofton Uniacke House, 5248 Morris Street

*I*n 1865 Edward W. Chipman, a prosperous dry goods merchant, and his wife of eight years, Mahala Jane, began to build their dream home. When completed, their handsome Italianate villa, with its pillared entrance and exotic pagoda-like bay windows, was deemed to be "more like a palace than a private residence". But alas, Chipman soon over-extended himself and the property was sold at a public auction in 1874 for $11,300.

Just two years later, however, the house entered its golden age as the Waverley Hotel under the capable management of Misses Sarah and Jane Romans. For thirty years the Romans sisters operated the respectable and popular establishment where "the guests feel they are actually guests".

Some of the paying guests were famous; Oscar Wilde stayed at the Waverley in October 1882 when he was invited to lecture at the Academy of Music. Longer-term patrons at the hotel were drawn from the upper echelons of Halifax society. Businessman John Doull resided at the Waverley Hotel from 1888 to 1898 while he was President of the Bank of Nova Scotia. Samuel H. Brookfield, the construction magnate, Robert Pickford of the Pickford and Black shipping line, and military chaplain, Rev. Norman Lee, were all boarders. Even Premier George H. Murray stayed six consecutive years while in office □

Plate 16. Sterling Hotel, 1264-1266 Barrington Street

JAIRUS HART HOUSE
1340 Barrington Street

SARAH MOREN
HOUSE
1334 Barrington Street

Situated side-by-side, these two brick houses are stylistic opposites. The Hart House, built in 1864, is a late example of the long-lasting Georgian style; the symmetrical plan, truncated pitched roof, Scottish oriel dormers and corner quoins are typical. In contrast, the Moren House was constructed in 1887, according to Victorian fashion trends. The French mansard roof, the bay window, the decorative brickwork and the segmental arches accenting the main doorway, all represent the Second Empire style.

Jairus Hart began business by shipping supplies to isolated ports in a boat he had built himself. And though he opted for a sedate traditional style of home, he was not above taking personal risks. He took the chance of postponing his wedding to follow a good run of fish, hoping his bride would accept him later as well as richer! She accepted and he prospered until his death in 1906 when his estate totalled almost half a million dollars.

The neighbouring Moren House was first owned and built by James R. Lithgow. Lithgow had developed several nearby properties and had been treasurer of the Glace Bay Mining Company. In 1893, Lithgow sold the house to the widowed Sarah Moren whose husband had served as president of the same mining company.

Both houses were eventually taken over by the Technical University of Nova Scotia, and by 1977

the Moren House was destined for demolition. Fortunately President Clair J. Callaghan pressed for its preservation and restoration. Today, as the official president's residence, and the scene of many social functions, the Moren House is an architectural ambassador for the gracious Victorian era in a technological age □

34

Plate 17. Jairus Hart House, 1340 Barrington Street (right) and Sarah Moren House, 1334 Barrington Street (left)

Built in 1891 for local hotel-owner Thomas Renner, this miniature chateau is a light-hearted, whimsical example of "the modern French style". Reminiscent of the fabled rural chateaux of the 17th century French nobility, the style was revived as an urban novelty by the lavish 19th century court of the Emperor Napoleon III and the Empress Eugénie of France.

The tall chimneys, the curvaceous flare of the mansard roof and the central tower with its ornamental round and pointed dormers are typical elements of French elegance. The classical arched windows on the large box-bays and matching dormers characterize the 19th century influence on the style.

It is fitting that this dwelling, like a doll-house from the fantasy world of French courtiers, was once owned by a man who was devoted to children and the benefits of toys and make-believe. Soon after the Children's Hospital opened in 1909 with just 16 cots, Dr. Michael Carney was appointed to the staff. This modest medical man spent almost 40 years caring for and curing sick children.

Dr. Carney recognized the childrens' desire for play and the therapeutic effects of happy hours spent with toys. A new hospital playroom was a "hope closest to his heart". On May 12, 1954, shortly after his death, an expanded playroom was dedicated to his memory □

Plate 18. Renner-Carney House, 1351 Barrington Street

OLD PRESBYTERIAN
MANSE

1359 Barrington Street

FRASER TERRACE

5172, 5176, 5178, 5182
Bishop Street

*A*t the corner of Barrington and Bishop streets stands a sedate stone house originally built as the manse for St. Matthew's Church.

In 1828, the Presbyterian congregation purchased the corner lot for £235 and hired Charles Dunbrack and Richard Scott to build the sturdy residence of native ironstone and sandstone. Scott was the Scottish stone mason who had acted as supervising architect for Province House a few years earlier.

George Munro Grant, minister of St. Matthew's from 1863 to 1877, was the last minister to inhabit the house. He distinguished himself as an eloquent preacher and author of *Ocean to Ocean,* an account of travels with Sir Sandford Fleming. Before Grant left to become principal of Queen's University in Kingston, a new brick manse was built next door.

The old stone manse was purchased by George P. Mitchell, a prosperous West India merchant who added the fashionable French mansard roof. In the 1880's, the corner room under the sloping mansard housed a bright young Dalhousie student, Lucy Maud Montgomery, who eventually gained fame as the author of *Anne of Green Gables.*

Behind the old Presbyterian manse are the four attached townhouses of Fraser Terrace. William Fraser, a piano manufacturer, built the terrace in 1862. As an attractive mid-Victorian variation on a Georgian theme, the two centre houses have

traditional Scottish oriel dormers, while both the easterly and westerly houses have oversize oriel dormers to match their Victorian wide-angled bay windows □

Plate 19.   Old Presbyterian Manse, 1359 Barrington Street (corner) and Fraser Terrace, 5172-5182 Bishop Street (left)

RUPERT GEORGE
House
1335 Hollis Street

GATE-YOUNG
HOUSE
1325 Hollis Street

At first glance these houses look like architectural twins; in fact they are more akin to parent and child. Rupert George, the Provincial Secretary, had his traditional Georgian townhouse with Scottish dormers built about 1835. Twenty years later, a neighbouring brick house appeared; like an offspring it was similar in design but grew to slightly larger proportions.

Subsequent owners of the Rupert George House included James Creighton, shipping merchant and ancestor of renowned folklorist Dr. Helen Creighton, as well as John P. Mott, the first manufacturer of chocolates in Canada.

The Gate-Young House was not named for its first owner, David Allison, but for John W. Young, a wealthy West India merchant, who purchased the house in 1859 for £3,025 and erected memorable wrought-iron gates beside it.

Early in this century the Gate-Young House was owned by the Honorable Humphrey Mellish, Judge of the Supreme Court of Nova Scotia and Judge in Admiralty. He was described by a colleague as a slight man with "a fine forehead and a dome-like Shakespearean head". He was witty and "one of the very few to keep up the study of Latin and Greek". He was a brilliant lawyer and a lenient judge; no one was ever convicted of a capital crime in his court □

Plate 20. Rupert George House, 1335 Hollis Street (left) and Gate-Young House, 1325 Hollis Street (right)

*T*he history of this sophisticated Italianate villa, with its decorative windows and fanciful "Romeo and Juliet" balcony, is linked with the risky undercover business of blockade-running during the American Civil War.

The house was built by Henry Peters for the Honourable Benjamin Wier, a consummate politician, merchant trader, and chief Confederate agent in Halifax. Described as a man of strong passions with "a great massive face with a remarkably sallow complexion and a harsh expression", Benjamin Wier and his company promoted the dangerous commerce with the blockaded Southern ports.

In 1864, Wier provisioned the *Tallahassee*, the famous Confederate raider that took refuge in Halifax harbour after sinking 50 northern merchant vessels. Under the laws of neutrality the vessel had only 48 hours to refuel and repair a broken mast before facing two Union cruisers which waited off Chebucto Head. According to Captain John Taylor Wood's account, B. Wier and Co. went "promptly on board and took energetic steps to meet our wants". The dramatic escape of the *Tallahassee* up the Eastern Passage in the dead of night must have pleased Benjamin Wier and all those that supported the Confederate cause in Halifax □

Plate 21.   Benjamin Wier House, 1459 Hollis Street

*A*lexander Keith was born in 1795 in Caithness-shire, Scotland. At the age of 17, he began his apprenticeship in his uncle's brewing business. By 1821, the mature 26-year old had not only emigrated to Halifax but had commenced his own brewery on Argyle Street; in the *Acadian Recorder* he advertised his "long experience" and his intention to brew "Strong Ales, Porter, Ginger Wine, Table and Spruce Beer". The following year, he took over a competitor, Charles Boggs, inheriting the "large and commodious brew house and premises in Lower Water Street".

The brewery expanded to keep pace with increasing demand for beer. Buildings for the grain stores, cooperage and brewing stages clustered comfortably around two inner cobblestone courtyards. Mysterious features like the church-like Gothic windows overlooking the upper courtyard were among the 19th century industrial refinements.

At the age of 68, Alexander Keith could afford to build a lavish new home on Hollis Street. The cornerstone was laid on September 2, 1863. Mrs. Eliza Keith "placed the first mortar, making use of a handsome silver trowel for the purpose". After three cheers for both the Queen and the host, the assembled workmen and guests were entertained "with roast-beef, plum pudding and XXX ale".

Designed by Scottish-born architect, William Hay, Keith Hall was the very model of an Italian Renais-

sance palazzo. The smooth, honey-coloured Wallace sandstone was decorated with expertly sculpted window surrounds; a pillared portico supporting a richly ornamented, urn-topped balustrade formed the grand entrance. The palatial theme was continued inside by the marble fireplaces, intricate cornices and exuberantly moulded doorways □

Plate 22. The Brewery Courtyard, Lower Water Street

Plate 23.   Keith Hall Portico, 1475 Hollis Street   *Plate 24.   Keith Hall Parlour Doorway, 1475 Hollis Street*

Governor John Wentworth and his socialite wife Frances emulated the grand lifestyle of the Wentworth nobility in Yorkshire. In 1799, Governor Wentworth persuaded the House of Assembly to build an official residence on the very site reserved for the proposed legislative building.

Soon the imposing front of Government House faced Hollis Street across a long lawn. Classical pilasters rose above the first storey, lateral wings added balance, and a curving staircase swept up to the main entrance. On the Barrington Street elevation the wings were fashionably bowed.

In 1808, Governor Sir George Prevost replaced Wentworth. Prevost had led a relatively spartan soldier's life since the age of 12, when he had joined his father's regiment, the 60th Foot. On arriving in Halifax, he was so shocked at such a large house that he immediately demanded, and got, an increase in salary! Prevost was fluent in French and "smooth and flattering in manner" — qualities which soon promoted him to the governorship for the whole of British North America. But he fell into disgrace after the War of 1812 when a naval court martial claimed his army's retreat at Plattsburgh had left the accompanying fleet to certain defeat.

Another military resident of Government House was the 51-year old Sir Peregrine Maitland, who served the dual role of Governor and Commander-in-Chief of the forces. At the age of 38, Maitland had ignored the strict propriety of the times and dared to elope with Lady Sarah Lennox, the lovely and already engaged 23-year old daughter of the powerful Duke of Richmond. But during Maitland's term in Halifax, moral conduct was uppermost in his mind. He always made a point of walking to church each week, and he publicly denounced the practice of going to market on Sundays!

One 20th-century Lieutenant-Governor, John Alexander Douglas McCurdy, was a pioneer of aviation. He joined F. W. Baldwin and Alexander Graham Bell in Baddeck, Nova Scotia. There, on February 23, 1909, he flew the Silver Dart and achieved the first controlled flight in the British Empire. He resided in Government House from 1947 to 1952.

Wentworth's magnificent Georgian mansion will admirably continue to house Nova Scotia's heads of state for centuries to come □

Plate 25. Government House, Hollis Street View

*T*he clean lines, tall chimneys and smooth-cut, granite-block front all contribute to the stately grandeur of this mansion. Its name is derived from two very different owners who lived in two very different eras.

John Black was a native of Greenock in Aberdeenshire, Scotland, and an active Georgian entrepreneur. As early as 1790, Black had secured a contract from the Admiralty to cut timber in New Brunswick for ships' masts. Between 1806 and 1811 he shared the contract with his brother William, before moving to Halifax and leaving William in charge at Saint John. In 1812, he was a co-owner of the *Caledonia*, the first Halifax vessel to be commissioned as a privateer for the ensuing war with the American colonies.

Privateering proved exceedingly lucrative; John Black spent some of his profits on construction of the fine Hollis Street mansion. Like his brother William who became mayor of Saint John, he went into politics and was named to Nova Scotia's Executive Council in 1813. Later his daughter, Rosina Jane, lived in the house with her husband, James Boyle Uniacke, who led a distinguished political life as Provincial Treasurer, Attorney General and Premier of the province.

A contrast to the life of John Black was the life of the Right Reverend Hibbert Binney, the pious Victorian bishop who inhabited the house for more than thirty years.

An Oxford scholar, Hibbert Binney was consecrated Bishop of Nova Scotia at the age of 31, in 1851. From the beginning he was against local laxities and "popular whims and fashions", but his unyielding and precise religious concepts ran into trouble.

One rector refused to relinquish his black gown for a white surplice, while another claimed that Binney contravened the precepts of the Protestant Reformation. However much he loathed the Calvinist leanings of his own clergy, he was not opposed to selling the land at the back of his house to the Presbyterians for St. Matthew's Church.

The youthful Bishop Binney was the only bishop to marry while in office. He espoused a Miss Mary Bliss and was reportedly very happy!

Plate 26. Black-Binney House, 1472 Hollis Street

ST. MATTHEW'S
CHURCH

Barrington Street at
Spring Garden Road

OLD COURT HOUSE

Spring Garden Road

The congregation of St. Matthew's United Church is the oldest Protestant dissenting congregation in Canada. Initially consisting of New England Congregationalists and Scottish Presbyterians, the congregation eventually became solidly Presbyterian. When fire consumed the first pioneer meeting house in 1857, a new site was acquired.

Members of the congregation who had visited Toronto, suggested the architectural firm of William Thomas and Sons. This firm made a specialty of churches, designing more than 30 in total and 12 in Toronto alone.

William Thomas had been born in Suffolk, England, and is believed to have been trained as an architect by Richard Tutin of Birmingham. In 1843 he emigrated to Toronto with his wife, Martha Tutin Thomas. The couple had ten children — four sons and six daughters. William Thomas was "a patient and loving father" who enjoyed playing chess, singing and dancing. Perhaps his numerous architectural commissions were due in part to "his kindly social qualities which endeared him to a numerous circle of friends".

By 1857 two of William Thomas' sons, William and Cyrus, both trained by their father, were partners in the flourishing firm. Cyrus Thomas designed St. Matthew's Church.

The finely-wrought Gothic exterior of the church, with buttresses, finials and crenellations, is contrasted by the interior. There, the three-sided gallery supported by round pillars and the primitive box pews contribute to an atmosphere of pioneer charm reminiscent of the early Congregationalist meeting house.

With the St. Matthew's commission the Thomas' firm was formally introduced to Halifax. In 1858, Cyrus Thomas entered and won the architectural competition to design the Court House.

The firm had an excellent record in designing significant public buildings, including the town halls in Niagara-on-the-Lake and Guelph, the district jail in Simcoe, the court house in Chatham, the custom house in Quebec, and the St. Lawrence Hall and Don Jail in Toronto.

Like the Halifax Court House, most of the public projects were won in competitions and had classical design features in common. The Court House is "visually powerful" with strong vermiculated stonework and massive banded columns beneath the pediment on the projecting frontispiece. Lions' heads and bearded human heads at the main entrance vigorously proclaim the solemnity and strength of the law. The Court House is believed to be the best example of the firm's bold Victorian public buildings □

Plate 27. St. Matthew's Church, 1479 Barrington Street

Plate 28. Old Court House, Spring Garden Road

William Critchlow Harris was a talented Maritime architect remembered for his many picturesque Gothic churches and Queen Anne houses throughout Prince Edward Island and Nova Scotia.

Indeed, Harris was very much a product of the two provinces. He grew up in Prince Edward Island after emigrating from Britain with his family at the age of two. He was trained as an architect in Halifax by David Stirling during a five-year apprenticeship from 1870 to 1875. Except for a two-year stay in Winnipeg, his entire career was centred in the Maritimes.

Like many highly creative people, Harris had a dreamy, introspective nature and no head for finances. He was a bachelor with a slim athletic build, thick dark hair and slightly rumpled "tweedy" clothes. Though he behaved cordially to people, he was considered an eccentric recluse. He loved to tramp through wilderness areas, often playing the flute as he went.

During the 1890's, Harris was constantly on the move between Prince Edward Island and Nova Scotia. In 1898, he opened an office in the Keith Building on Barrington Street. About that time he began to design houses that looked like castles with round towers topped by elongated conical roofs; one such house was imprinted on his business card as his trademark. Other signatures of his Romantic style were hipped gabled roofs derived from European peasant cottages and enclosed grotto-like verandas. He also favoured surface enrichment like small corner buttresses and "fishscale" shingles for the second storey. Harris was an innovator; he was bold enough to mix diverse elements from baronial castles, peasant cottages and mysterious grottos to produce workable, personal designs for comfortable middle-class houses. The Robie Street house is an excellent ambassador of the Harris style, incorporating each of his special effects.

Robert Harris, a brother and noted portrait-painter, aptly related William Harris' lifestyle to his architecture: "He lived in such a dream world ... there is much of it in the buildings he designed. They are dreams in timber, brick and stone."□

Plate 29.   William Critchlow Harris House, 1328 Robie Street

MacDonald
Library

Studley Campus,
Dalhousie University

Oakville

1460 Oxford Street

Professor Charles MacDonald, who had taught mathematics at Dalhousie University for almost 40 years, died on March 11, 1901. He left Dalhousie $2,000 "for the purchase of books, chiefly in English literature".

Library space in the all-purpose Forrest Building was already cramped. Thus the need for a new library building coincided with the desire to commemorate the popular professor. A fund-raising campaign was launched and within three months more than $16,000 of the required $20,000 was pledged for the MacDonald Memorial Library.

An architectural competition was announced with a prize of $100 for the best design. Four sets of plans were submitted and examined, but all were rejected by the Board of Governors. This bottleneck was further complicated by the search for a proper site.

Almost a decade of delay followed while library conditions became intolerable. The establishment of the School of Dentistry meant that books had to be relegated to the faculty lounge and the attic of the Forrest Building. Finally, in 1911 the widowed Elizabeth Murray, whose husband had been a friend of President Forrest, sold her 41-acre property to Dalhousie for the reasonable sum of $50,000.

The cornerstone for the MacDonald Library, the first building on the new campus, was laid on April 24, 1914. Architect for the project was Andrew Randall Cobb, a New Yorker who had been in Halifax only four years. Cobb had studied at the Ecole des Beaux Arts in Paris and travelled extensively in Britain, France and Italy. For the design of the library he drew from the formal classical repertoire — the pillared portico, the grand Palladian window, the central pediment. The effect of these regular, dignified elements set in the irregular, dark native ironstone, is striking.

By the summer of 1915 the MacDonald Library was in use, and the 20th century building boom that would eventually fill the new Studley campus had begun. Along with the construction of new buildings, the rapidly expanding University also purchased many houses and buildings in the immediate neighbourhood. Some were used for offices, others for extra classrooms, and one, Oakville, became the President's house.

Just as Dalhousie College was founded on the spoils of the War of 1812, Oakville had sprung from the profits of the American Civil War. Shipping merchant, Levi Hart participated in the trade with the blockaded southern states and made his fortune. In 1866 and 1867 he acquired the land on Oxford Street and soon inhabited his expansive new mansion. Its style reflects both Hart's wealth and his sea-going business ventures. The rounded, mullioned windows, bracketed cornice and balustraded porch suggest an Italian villa while the "widow's walk" cupola is a reminder of his dependence on the sea.

Plate 30.   MacDonald Library, Dalhousie University

The location and magnificence of Levi Hart's house made it a perfect candidate for a president's house. The $25,000 for the purchase was donated in 1925 by a member of the Board of Governors, Richard Bedford Bennett.

A native of New Brunswick, Bennett had graduated from Dalhousie Law School in 1893. While practising law in Calgary he had entered politics. In 1921, he inherited a ready-made fortune from his long-time friend Jennie Shirreff Eddy, wife of E. B. Eddy, the millionaire match manufacturer.

From 1930 to 1935 he served as Prime Minister of Canada, but his personal wealth did not endear him to the people during the years of the Great Depression. His overbearing and unforgiving personality did not help his image either. In fact, R. B. Bennett was called "the most vindictive man ever to be Prime Minister". But his unpopularity was at least matched by his generosity. Though he was frequently alone at Christmas, he regularly sent out 100 floral gifts and 25 dozen boxes of candies. And his donations to Dalhousie totalled $762,000!

Plate 31. Oakville, 1460 Oxford Street

OLD TOWN

*E*nos Collins was born in Liverpool, Nova
Scotia, the second child of Hallet Collins
whose three wives produced a total of 26
children. Young Enos earned his keep by going to
sea on one of his father's trading vessels; before he
reached the age of 20, he was bound for Bermuda
as captain of the schooner *Adamant*.

Throughout the 97-year voyage of his life, Enos
Collins remained adamant in his quest for profit and
power. During the Napoleonic Wars, three of his
ships, laden with supplies for the beleaguered British
Army, successfully broke through a naval blockade
off the coast of Cadiz, Spain. Remuneration for the
daring exploit was high and Collins soon set himself
up in business in Halifax. During the War of 1812, his
three privateers, including the legendary *Liverpool
Packet*, terrorized the New England coastline; captured American vessels were brought to Halifax and
their rich cargoes eagerly sold.

After the war, Collins combined currency speculation
with his mercantile ventures. He became the dominant, founding partner in the Halifax Banking
Company, the city's first bank. The bank became
known as Collins' Bank as its premises were located
in Collins' ironstone warehouse, built in 1823.

Much to Enos Collins' displeasure the bank's monop-
oly did not last. In 1832, a charter was granted to the
Bank of Nova Scotia and by 1864, the appearance of
three more banks caused one journalist to comment in

disbelief, "If there is enough for all of them to do,
their existence indicates extraordinary prosperity."
One of the newcomers was a "popular moneyed
institution", the People's Bank, with new headquarters at the corner of Duke and Hollis streets.

One hundred years later, the fate of the People's Bank
Building and neighbouring structures along Hollis
and Granville streets was precarious. Enos Collins'
Bank and Warehouse and six adjacent buildings
on Privateers' Wharf sat vacant and derelict behind
a chain-link fence; the city's engineering department was preparing to demolish the whole group.
Fronting on the narrow Upper Water Street, the
hapless structures were directly in the path of
Harbour Drive, a proposed waterfront expressway.

In an effort to save the buildings, the Heritage Trust
of Nova Scotia, a volunteer citizens' society, raised
public support. Halifax City Council appointed an
Advisory Committee on Historic Preservation which
presented persuasive briefs to the elected representatives. Faculty members of the Nova Scotia College
of Art and Design creatively proposed a new downtown campus in the old structures. Parks Canada
designated the seven waterfront buildings as a
National Historic Site.

In spite of these positive actions the dreaded moment
came when the demolition crew and heavy machinery arrived at Privateers' Wharf. The wrecking

Plate 32. Collins' Bank and Warehouse, Privateers' Wharf

machine struck forcefully against Enos Collins' warehouse. But the old structure withstood the brunt of the assault without damage. The demolition crew were so awed by the strength of the stones that they withdrew the ineffectual equipment.

At last, Mayor Allan O'Brien and City Council sided with public opinion. Harbour Drive was stopped. Instead, the restoration project of local developer John Fiske went ahead. The Nova Scotia College of Art and Design happily occupies 21 buildings. And Historic Properties is one of the country's greatest attractions □

Plate 33. People's Bank and neighbouring buildings, Corner of Duke and Hollis Streets

On the night of September 9, 1859, fire raged in downtown Halifax, destroying 60 buildings including all of the wooden shops on Granville Street. But disaster was soon turned into opportunity and a magnificent masonry streetscape rose from the ashes.

Like great Renaissance tapestries on each side of the street, the pillars, pilasters and pediments, keystones, crests and corbels, are woven into the patterns of rhythmic arches — Norman, Romanesque and Venetian Gothic. The individuality of the shops within the harmony of the whole composition was largely achieved by Cyrus Pole Thomas of William Thomas & Sons of Toronto, one of the most active architectural firms before Confederation. Cyrus Thomas, one of the "sons" of the enterprising firm, established his own branch office in Halifax while working on the Granville Street project.

Shops along the fashionable thoroughfare sold "many of the richest specimens of the world's manufacture" — muslins, millinery, hoop skirts and "black cloth sacque coats" as well as hand-crafted silverware, the latest books from London, 40 varieties of boots, and shoes in 230 different styles.

Presently, the upper storeys of the restored buildings on the east side comprise the campus of the Nova Scotia College of Art and Design. On the west side, the stones of the facade were dismantled in 1978 and then, like a jig-saw puzzle, fitted back into place over a new structure.

In the days before new-fangled power-driven buggies, horses took advantage of the ornate Victorian water trough; small dishes near the bottom of the trough offered relief for thirsty dogs □

Plate 34. *Granville Streetscape*

OLD BANK OF
COMMERCE
5171 George Street

OLD MERCHANTS'
BANK OF CANADA
1819 Granville Street

*I*n 1823 Halifax's first bank (Collins' Bank) was distinguishable from neighbouring warehouses only by its heavy security door topped by the word BANK. By the late 19th and early 20th centuries, however, banks traded on their architectural styles more than any other commercial or industrial business.

In 1906, the Bank of Commerce was constructed in an imposing Greek Temple style. Four massive stone scroll-capped pillars supported a moulded entablature surmounted by a triangular pediment heavily grooved with dentils. Customers who entered the bank through this portico, symbolic of power and stability, were reassured.

In 1911, the Montreal architectural firm of Hogle and Davis made use of the richly decorated Italianate style for the Merchants' Bank. Rising from a foundation of Terence Bay granite, ten tall pilasters with ornate Corinthian capitals lead the eye upward past arched windows to the intricate cornices and elegant rooftop balustrade. Customers appreciated the palatial ornamentation, symbolic of great wealth.

Ironically, in the latter half of the 20th century, many banks and trust companies have spurned architectural individuality and symbolism. In their haste to show a modern image they have occupied nondescript high-rise office towers that are only distinguishable by their high-placed neon insignia □

Plate 35. Old Bank of Commerce, 5171 George Street

Plate 36.   Old Merchants' Bank of Canada, 1819 Granville Street

One 19th century Nova Scotia newspaper editor claimed that newspapers "always increase with the intelligence of the people". The collective intelligence quotient of the populace of Nova Scotia between 1840 and 1867 was not determined, but if the editor's statement was true, the resulting score might have been superhumanly high. For during that time span, the province was a hotbed of journalistic fervor — a grand total of 80 different newspapers reached the reading public!

One of the longest-running newspapers was the *Acadian Recorder*, in existence from 1813 to 1930. So keen was its founding editor, Anthony Henry Holland, to scoop competitors, that he would row out to vessels as they arrived in port, to glean the latest news.

Anthony Holland modelled the *Recorder* on London's celebrated *Political Register* which regularly exposed the politicians' misdemeanors for public scrutiny. In fact, the *Acadian Recorder* was the first Nova Scotia newspaper to officially criticize the all-powerful Tory government. Years later in the 1850's, however, the *Recorder* became more Conservative when the political patronage of the Liberal administration conflicted with the paper's principles of "fairness and impartiality".

The turn-of-the-century Acadian Recorder Building was home to the newspaper during its last three decades of operation. Like the reform paper with traditional principles, the predominantly classical, yellow brick building with traditional pilasters and rooftop balustrade, is enlivened by bevelled central windows which add an appropriate avant-garde air □

Plate 37. Acadian Recorder Building, 1724 Granville Street

*T*he beginnings of this magnificent government edifice were fraught with innuendo, financial failure and political deadlock.

In 1863, architect David Stirling, fresh from his triumph at the Halifax Club, prepared plans for the new post office and customs building. This design was a virtuoso performance in the classical Italianate style.

But before construction began, insinuations were aired in the press. When George Lang's construction bid was too speedily selected, there were veiled charges of collusion. Both Lang and Stirling had come from Rosburghshire, in Scotland, and had jointly operated the Albert Freestone Quarries in New Brunswick in the 1850's.

George Lang was well-known in Halifax as a sculptor, stone mason and builder. He had collaborated with Stirling in building the Halifax Club and had been solely responsible for several Granville Street buildings. But the popular highlight of his career was his life-size lion atop the Sebastopol monument in the Old Burying Ground.

In hindsight, George Lang might well have wished he had not tackled the post office. His troubles began in the spring of 1864 when both carpenters and stone-cutters went on strike. Then costs rose when extra freestone was needed from Pictou County and extra machinery to cope with the oversize stone

blocks was imported from the United States. Finally, with his credit over-extended, Lang was forced to declare bankruptcy and retreat to a low-profile life of brick-making in Shubenacadie, Nova Scotia.

A second contractor, John Brookfield, completed the building in 1868, just one year after Confederation. However, under the new political format, post offices had become a federal responsibility. When Ottawa claimed the costly structure, the first federal-provincial dispute raged. The building remained empty until 1871 when Nova Scotia exacted payment of $80,000, half the cost of construction, from the federal government.

Presently, the Old Post Office houses the Art Gallery of Nova Scotia □

Plate 38. Old Post Office, Cheapside and Bedford Row

*T*he cornerstone of Province House was ceremoniously laid on August 12, 1811, by Governor Sir George Prevost who poured corn, wine and oil over it to symbolize prosperity, and then with three strokes of the hammer, proclaimed: "May the building that shall rise from this foundation perpetuate the Loyalty and Liberality of the Province of Nova Scotia."

It is not difficult to espouse such high ideals upon entering the magnificent Red Chamber. The profusion and intricacy of the ornamentation would prove uplifting to even the most downcast soul. The tall windows, outlined with chains of decorative loops and rosettes, are surmounted by ornate entablatures where rose and acorn motifs entwine with thistles, lions' heads and smoothly-moulded shells. The walls are embellished with panels of bold swags and delicate bells; at intervals fluted Corinthian pilasters appear to support the lofty canopied ceiling handsomely festooned with lacy plasterwork.

Perhaps more amazing than the perfection of the Georgian decor is the very fact that such a stylish legislature was constructed at all. After decades of delay, switching and re-switching the site, passing parliamentary Acts, and striking and re-striking government committees, Province House was finally achieved. The design was produced by John Merrick who was not an architect but an influential contractor who sold paint, varnish and turpentine in great quantities to the Navy and Army for their wooden ships and barracks. The supervising architect was Richard Scott, a 29-year old Scottish stone mason, who likely prepared the working drawings, dealt with the numerous contractors, and even provided the stone from his quarry on the banks of the Wallace River.

Merrick's vision, Scott's expertise and the gargantuan and meticulous efforts of many contractors have given Nova Scotia a sumptuous architectural prize. It is as true today as in 1819 when Province House was completed, that there is "scarcely a building on this side of the Atlantic, in which elegance and accommodation are more happily combined"□

Plate 39. Red Chamber, Province House

At a time when the Canadian economy was struggling to rebound from the Great Depression, the directors and shareholders of the Bank of Nova Scotia decided at their 99th Annual Meeting on January 28, 1931, to finance the construction of a new head office. The eminent, Irish-born Canadian architect, John Lyle, was chosen for the costly $800,000 project.

Lyle, who had studied at Yale and the Ecole des Beaux Arts in Paris, was at the peak of his career. During a period of confusing stylistic debate among proponents of elaborate British Victorian idioms or starkly functional International designs, John Lyle sought a distinctive Canadian architecture with meaningful regional decoration.

The site of the new bank, opposite Province House, was very important to Lyle. He felt that "certain characteristics of this very fine building should be echoed in the new building". Thus, traditional pilasters rising above rusticated or channelled stonework recall the style of Province House; from these basic classical decorations, Lyle progressed with his personal design.

In his own words, Lyle described his original decorative symbols as "eighty-six different Canadian motifs from the small trailing arbutus — the floral emblem of Nova Scotia — to the sunflower, and from the seagull to the Canada goose ". Indeed, pairs of bears, geese and seahorses are carved in stone while codfish dance on the wrought-iron window grilles. The exquisite bronze gates to the safety deposit department are an intricate filigree of tulips, corn, maple leaves, beavers, gulls and squirrels.

The 30-foot high ceiling of the magnificent banking hall is replete with octagonal recessed "coffers" showing stylized heads of Neptune with water lilies, swans, foxes and ducks. Even the world of industry and commerce was not excluded from Lyle's repertoire. Stone panels on the exterior Prince Street facade depict both the workings of the Sydney steel plant and the beauty of a clipper ship in full sail. Emblazoned on the central frieze beneath the roof cornice, are mammoth Canadian coins.

The foresight of the bank's directors and the profuse creativity of John Lyle have produced "as complex and rich a building as has ever been built in this country"□

Plate 40.   Bank of Nova Scotia, 1709 Hollis Street

The New Year's Day fire of 1857 was devastating; the heat was so intense that the hair and whiskers of the volunteer fire-fighters were singed and the hand-operated engine finally "burned up where it stood on the street".

It took ten years to replace the wooden buildings that had been consumed by the inferno on Prince and Hollis streets. By the early 1860's three complementary brick buildings climbed the steep slope of Prince Street. The central structure of the trio housed Joseph Howe's newspaper, the *Novascotian*. Howe, who had fought and won freedom of the press, wrote rousing editorials denouncing Confederation as the "Botheration Scheme". His efforts were countered by next door neighbours on both sides. The *British America Union* newspaper in the Heffernan Building was "the official organ of the Union League" and Samuel Leonard Shannon, an occupant of the Geldert Building was granted the title "Honourable" by Queen Victoria in recognition of his strong stand in favour of Confederation.

While the occupants of the three brick buildings were in the forefront of Victorian political movements, the chief occupant of the "handsome freestone building" at the corner was in the forefront of a movement that did not become a burning issue until the 20th century — women's liberation. In 1867 Sarah Howard, an independant entrepreneur, opened a new department store in her luxurious Italianate structure.

Though she looked like Queen Victoria in her voluminous gown and lace head-dress, Sarah Howard was an astute and daring business woman. She used a "spirited and skilful system of advertising" and her firm was the first to employ commercial travellers in the Maritimes.

Sarah Howard sold goods of high fashion and quality like "French kid gloves", "rich Irish poplins" and "Maltese lace sets". Her Millinery Show Room on the second floor was a vision of parasols, bonnets, flowers and feathers which prompted one observer to note, "No wonder the daughters of fashion make haste to offer their devotions at this shrine!"□

Plate 41. Prince Streetscape

*T*hese adjacent structures have witnessed many decades from a similar vantage point, but they are widely separated in age, function and style.

In 1862 when the ornate Italianate Halifax Club was under construction, the simple, 30-year old pitched-roof Georgian shop next door was operating as the London Drug Store. Inside, druggist George Johnson offered Langley's Cordial Rhubarb, Godfrey's Extract of Elder Flowers and Leake's Persian Odonto, Myrrh and Borax. Other "standard articles" included brushes, trusses and even leeches!

Architect for the Halifax Club was David Stirling, a native of Galashiels, Scotland, who came to Halifax via St. John's, Newfoundland, where he had designed a bank, and Toronto where he had worked on Osgoode Hall. His design for the respectable gentlemen's club was highly acclaimed by the London press which commented on the carvings of female busts embellished with fruit and flowers. Ironically, no real women were permitted membership until more than a century had passed.

The club's clientele included the city's most influential men — politicians, merchants and bankers. Both King George V and King Edward VIII, when still princes, attended gala celebrations at the Halifax Club.

Probably a few of the worthies, bellies overstuffed with Victorian ducks, puddings and port, dropped into the London Drug Store for a bottle of Cockle's Antibilious Pills or Langley's Tooth Ache Tincture □

Plate 42. *London Drug Store, 1674 Hollis Street (left) and Halifax Club, 1682 Hollis Street (right)*

Saint Paul's Anglican Church is a landmark of both the city's and the nation's architectural heritage. Constructed in the spring and summer of 1750, St. Paul's was the first public building in the newly-founded garrison town of Halifax. Today, the pioneer church is recognized as the oldest Protestant church in Canada.

The structure is a masterly combination of early building techniques of the New World and refined classical design of the Old Country. St. Paul's was modelled on James Gibbs' drawings of Marybone Chapel (now St. Peter's Vere Street) in London, England. Gibbs had trained both in Rome with Vatican architect, Carolo Fontana, and in London with the celebrated master of church architecture, Sir Christopher Wren. With the publication of his drawings, Gibbs' personal fame and influence at least equalled that of his teachers.

St. Paul's is the very essence of James Gibbs' style — the pure classical simplicity of the main structure and the contrasting decorative flourish of a three-tiered baroque steeple. But unlike its brick ancestor in London, St. Paul's is an example of the ingenious methods and typical materials used by North America's early builders. The pine timbers and oak frame were prefabricated in Boston and shipped to Halifax. About 30,000 bricks were made locally for the brick "nogging" or infill for the spaces between the main framing timbers of the exterior walls.

St. Paul's is illustrious from top to bottom. In the 20 burial vaults beneath the church, there are six former Governors of Nova Scotia, the Province's first Anglican Bishop, an 18th century Baron, a Vice-Admiral and two Generals!

Plate 43.   St. Paul's Church, Grand Parade

City Hall stands at the north end of the Grand Parade, the symbolic centre of Halifax. This perfectly appropriate position was only achieved after 12 years of controversy. On July 15, 1874, City Council decided on a site between Lockman and Poplar Grove streets owned by J. R. Jennett. But citizens who attended a public meeting a few days later were strongly opposed to this site. However, the majority of aldermen refused to revoke their decision and an agreement of purchase was drawn up for Mr. Jennett's land. Fortunately, Mayor John Sinclair was equally adamant in his own refusal to sign the agreement against the wishes of the citizens.

The south end of the Grand Parade in front of St. Paul's Church was also suggested as a suitable site. Naturally the Church rejected such an idea and influenced the House of Assembly to forbid the city from using the Grand Parade.

Nevertheless the citizenry still favoured the Grand Parade. Years later the city entered into negotiations with Dalhousie College for their property at the north end of the parade square. Dalhousie refused to accept the city's final offer of $25,000 plus a parcel of land. But Sir William Young saved the day with an additional $20,000 donation to Dalhousie contingent on their relinquishing the property.

A design competition with a prize of $300 was won by Edward Elliot, a local architect and native of Dartmouth. His winning design combined the classical formality of side pavilions, central portico and pediments with the spirited lightness of gabled dormers and a tall slender clock tower.

On August 18, 1888, the cornerstone was laid with a tap of Mayor O'Mullin's silver mounted mallet. Less than two years later, the contractors, Rhodes, Curry & Co., had completed the stone edifice. The grand opening took place on the lovely spring evening of May 22, 1890. Coloured lights were strung through the trees on the Grand Parade and a regimental band of the 63rd Halifax Rifles played in the second storey of the tower. Inside, more than 1,000 admiring guests were greeted by Mayor David MacPherson in the Council Chamber, and then treated to the rare delicacies of chocolate and ice-cream on the third floor.

Since that convivial occasion, City Hall has witnessed almost a century of democracy in action; the sites and styles of new buildings are still hotly debated within its walls □

Plate 44.   City Hall, Grand Parade

Barrington Street is the namesake of the 2nd Viscount Barrington of Ardglass, William Wildman Barrington, who rose to the Irish peerage in 1734. For many years Viscount Barrington served as Secretary of War in the British Cabinet. Appropriately, Barrington Street was associated with military manoeuvres in its early years. For example, on June 1, 1753, a proclamation ordered the militia from the south suburbs to muster within the palisade opposite the end of Barrington Street — approximately where Spring Garden Road intersects today. As well, the Grand Parade on Barrington was the old drilling ground for the militia and regular troops of the garrison.

Barrington Street is also associated with novel modes of transportation. In 1794, sedan chairs were hired on Barrington at a cost of one to two shillings; business was especially brisk in spring when the unpaved streets were ankle-deep in sloppy mud!

In spite of this early transportation venture, Barrington Street was not then the city's principal commercial thoroughfare. For well over 100 years commercial activity was concentrated on the lower streets. By 1822, a list of taxpayers and property values for Barrington Street included owners of residential properties plus a few businesses — a saddlery, a soap chandlery, a butcher and a tinsmith. Interestingly, the property with the highest assessed value, £7000, was that of Thomas Forrester's drygoods business.

Thomas Forrester's retail business was located in his new stone commercial building on the west side of Barrington, south of Prince Street. Forrester's drygoods trade continued throughout the 1820's and 1830's. By 1858, the sturdy ironstone and sandstone structure was occupied by William Fraser and Sons, "manufacturers of first class grand, square, oblique and cottage piano-fortes" and dealers for imported "cabinet organs and melodeons". Today the Forrester Building is the oldest commercial building on Barrington Street and one of very few Georgian shops in the city. And amazingly, one can still buy pianos from Phinney's Limited, a firm that has occupied the premises since 1912.

By 1870, transportation along Barrington Street had changed radically. William O'Brien had launched the first mass transit system — horse-drawn streetcars that ran on rails. While one reporter thought the Halifax City Railroad gave the city "an air of progress", the wealthier citizens, who rode in their own barouches and phaetons, despised the tracks that made riding on the cobblestone streets too bumpy for delicate posteriors!

Regardless of the opposing views on public transportation, the role of Barrington Street was becoming increasingly commercial. In 1872 the handsome, stuccoed brick Colwell Building was built; the continuous moulding outlining the round-headed windows gave the impression of an elegant Italian arcade. From 1890 to 1893 the "Bon Marche" millinery shop shared the ground floor with Reynolds gentlemen's furnish-

Plate 45.   Forrester Building, 1678 Barrington Street

Plate 46.   Colwell Building, 1673 Barrington Street

ings shop, while the Halifax Commercial College occupied the top floors. By 1901 Colwell Brothers' luxury clothing store had begun its 75-year tenure.

Of the same 1870's vintage and similar Italianate style is the small brick Cleverdon Building. The continuous moulding above the segmental window arches provides a strong architectural link to the Colwell Building. William Cleverdon was a watchmaker who carried on his artistic craft in the building from 1878 to 1903. Later in this century, the diminutive structure served as the retail outlet and studio of the renowned marine photographer Wallace MacAskill. Hardly a Nova Scotian home is without a hand-tinted view of Peggy's Cove, a scene of working fishermen in their dory or "My Ship of Dreams", the romantic rendering of a vessel in full sail!

In the late 1890's the public transportation network changed again. Poles were erected along the routes and overhead wires were strung. On February 12, 1896, the first electric tramcar made its trial run. The posh vehicle, propelled by two twenty-five horsepower motors, had mohair upholstery, quartered oak panelling and shiny bronze fittings. The tramcar manufacturer was the versatile firm that had constructed numerous Halifax buildings including City Hall itself — Rhodes, Curry & Company of Amherst, Nova Scotia.

Indeed, it was during the last decade of the 19th century and the early years of the 20th century that

Barrington Street finally reached its zenith as the city's main street. Many buildings, both commercial and institutional, were constructed — some flamboyant, others more modest, some grand at six storeys, others more traditional at three storeys.

A pleasant example of a modest building is the Harrison Building, built in 1893 for Harrison Brothers, retailers of interior decorating supplies and services. The brick and sandstone structure was probably designed by architect Edward Elliott, the designer of City Hall; the fan-shaped decoration under the roofed parapet was also used on the gables at City Hall. Elliott maintained an office in the building until after the turn-of-the-century.

A technically interesting double shop is the Brander Morris Building, constructed about 1907 for the furniture and upholstery business of two partners. With its sharply-pointed central gables and rough-textured surface, the facade is reminiscent of medieval Gothic styles, but the "stonework" is a modern invention. The exterior walls are, in fact, 12-inch thick concrete, artfully applied to resemble genuine stone!

Though diesel buses have replaced electric tramcars, the vintage architecture remains. The four central blocks of Barrington Street, from Spring Garden Road to George Street, constitute one of the longest and most fascinating heritage streetscapes in Canada □

Plate 47. *Cleverdon Building,*
            1711 Barrington Street

Plate 48. *Harrison Building,*
            1650 Barrington Street

Plate 49. *Brander Morris Building, 1566 Barrington Street*

THREE VICTORIAN
INSTITUTIONS

CITY CLUB
1580 Barrington Street

CHURCH OF
ENGLAND INSTITUTE
1588 Barrington Street

ST. MARY'S
YOUNG MEN'S
TOTAL ABSTINENCE
AND BENEVOLENT
SOCIETY
1572 Barrington Street

*T*hree adjacent "institutions" form an extraordinary architectural group on Barrington Street. The rich and varied details of the complementary brick structures provide a showcase of ornate High Victorian style.

The site of the Victorian trio was the large estate owned by the Honourable Simon Bradstreet Robie from 1823 to 1858. In fact, the central edifice was Robie's Georgian mansion. Simon Robie was a Massachusetts-born Loyalist whose long political career encompassed the high offices of Solicitor General and President of the Legislative Council. The City Club, a fashionable retreat for young men "belonging to the best families of Halifax", moved into the mansion in 1886. Members congregated to play billiards, read magazines like *Puck, Pall Mall* and *Empire*, dine elegantly, or even take a bath! In 1887, one member complained about the quality of the champagne; later complaints caused the charge for baths to drop from 25 to 15 cents.

In 1888, the northern third of the old Robie estate was sold for $2,250 to the Church of England Institute, which had been established 14 years earlier to encourage discussion among churchmen and to "diffuse a knowledge of the church's work". Because of a legacy from the wealthy and aristocratic Bishop Hibbert Binney, the churchmen could afford a fine site and building. Architect Henry Busch designed the new Institute for a fee of $600 and contractor John Cawsey carried out the construction for $12,218.

Born and educated in Europe, Henry Busch was well versed in traditional European styles. For the Institute, he conceived a highly decorative Gothic composition with an eye-catching suspended side spire. Bishop Binney would have been pleased with the design as he actively promoted the adoption of the Gothic style for church buildings.

By the spring of 1891 the southern portion of the old Robie estate was occupied by the "splendid new building of St. Mary's Young Men's Total Abstinence and Benevolent Society". The group, a Roman Catholic counterpart of the Protestant Young Men's Christian Association, hosted a successful grand opening in their superb quarters; 900 guests attended, Amerino's band played and non-alcoholic refreshments were served. One reporter quipped: "With the Church of England Institute on one side and St. Mary's Total Abstinence and Benevolent Society on the other, the City Club should find itself so girt about with temperance that the very champagne corks will be afraid to pop!"

Architect for the St. Mary's Total Abstinence and Benevolent Society was James Charles Dumaresq who had also designed the new Victorian front with three-storey box-bay windows for the City Club. Dumaresq was a native of Cape Breton and had studied the mechanics and concepts of architecture at Acadia University. His career was exemplary in its scope; he designed buildings throughout the province and in Bermuda. In New Brunswick he obtained the

Plate 50. *St. Mary's Young Men's Total Abstinence and Benevolent Society, 1572 Barrington (left),*
   City Club, 1580 Barrington Street (centre) and Church of England Institute, 1588 Barrington Street (right)

prestigious commission to design the provincial legislature. Undoubtedly, his eminent stature as an architect was due to the incredible diversity of his styles. Dumaresq's buildings are difficult to categorize as each is quite different from any others.

To unify the Barrington Street trio, Dumaresq maintained the general rhythm of fenestration with pairs of decorative, arched windows for the temperance society's building. The central tower projection adds verticality and complements the tall box-bays of the City Club and the spire of the Church of England Institute. The roof type is also perfectly in keeping with the mansard roofs of the neighbouring institutions — yet it is entirely unique in Halifax! While the City Club and the Church of England Institute have concave mansards, the St. Mary's Total Abstinence and Benevolent Society building has a bulbous convex mansard roof.

The unusually roofed structure has also had a long life as a movie theatre. The Nickle, Halifax's first permanent movie house, opened on May 3, 1907. In 1941, inflation may have been responsible for the name change to The Imperial. Still later, the name of the movie house became The Family. Films may still be enjoyed on the premises, now regional office of the National Film Board. And often the admission fee, better than at the old Nickle, is a modern taxpayers' miracle — free!

Plate 51.   Church of England Institute, 1588 Barrington Street

*T*he picturesque, almost fairy-tale quality of these Gothic buildings is refreshing in the precise and functional worlds of commerce and medicine.

The Smith Building was constructed in 1893 for George M. Smith & Company, a well-established drygoods firm that marketed "super waterproofs", parasols and ladies garments including "wool, silk, and cambric underwear". Local architect James Charles Dumaresq collaborated with a New Brunswick colleague, Harry H. Mott, on the intriguing design of the building. The two men were well-acquainted as Dumaresq had spent 10 years working in Saint John after the disastrous fire of 1877. His Nova Scotia partnership with Harry Mott was short-lived, however, as Mott returned to Saint John after only two years.

While the bay windows and segmental arches are borrowed from other styles, the gabled parapet and imposing finials rising above the roofline create an overall Gothic impression. The combination of smooth and rough-textured dark stonework also add to the Gothic character of the structure.

The smaller-scale Kaiser Building was built about the same time for dentist Edmund P. Ennis. The Gothic overtones are produced by the sharply pointed central gable and the rugged, turret-like bartizans along each side of the upper storeys. As well, the polychromy or multi-coloured effect is derived from the Gothic tradition. The use of yellow glazed brick and white granite in geometric patterns is a colourful contrast to the dark granite.

Edmund Ennis' dentistry practice, and Smith's drygoods firm provided their professional and commercial services from their respective buildings for more than 30 years. Both buildings share the distinction of being among the last commercial buildings to be built of stone before brick became the dominant construction material.□

Plate 52. Smith Building, 1715 Barrington Street (right)
Kaiser Building, 1723 Barrington Street (left)

Revolutionary changes in architecture and construction technology evolved in the extensive rebuilding after the Chicago fire of 1871. The development of steel beam construction meant that exterior walls were no longer load-bearing. A steel frame could support a much higher structure than heavy masonry walls; brick or stone cladding could be applied to the steel frame like clapboard and shingles to the frame of a wooden house. Windows could be larger as the ratio of glass to brick or stone was no longer critical for structural stability.

The ultimate result of the new technology was to be the steel and glass highrise of the 20th century — utilitarian in style and completely out of scale with the human context. But in the early years of the 1880's and 1890's the Chicago style of architecture was still highly decorative and building heights were relatively modest, particularly in the smaller urban centres.

In fact, the showy new designs and slightly higher proportions were perfectly suited to commercial buildings. In Halifax, Barrington Street was the up-to-date commercial thoroughfare of the gay nineties; several Chicago-style buildings attest to that fact.

Local architect Edward Elliot, fresh from his triumph with the prestigious City Hall, designed a Chicago-style building for the Nova Scotia Furnishing Com-

pany. The six-storey structure had all the "sheer commercial splendour" of its larger Chicago counterparts — a vast expanse of glass under broad Romanesque arches and a typical flurry of small arched windows and cornice brackets geared to raise the architectural tempo as the eye of the beholder travelled upward. When completed on September 24, 1894, the building was hailed as the "largest and finest furniture and carpet warehouse in the Dominion". The *Morning Chronicle* noted that "the plate glass windows are the largest in the city" and the whole structure "towers above all others on Barrington Street and looks like a giant among so many pigmies". The tall building also boasted a concurrent technological invention, the "passenger elevator" which promised to take you "to the top of the building where a fine view of the city is obtained".

In 1896 George Wright, entrepreneur and developer, commissioned James Charles Dumaresq to design the adjacent Wright Building. Wright had made his money compiling and publishing handy catalogues and guide books. For example, he published the world's first trade directory entitled "Wright's World Directory". The directory was distributed worldwide by the renowned Lloyd's Insurance Company. He then invested a quarter of a million dollars in Halifax real estate and developed numerous houses in the south suburbs including those on Wright Avenue and his own on Young Avenue as well as two commercial buildings on Barrington Street.

Plate 53. Nova Scotia Furnishing Company, 1668 Barrington Street (left)
Wright Building, 1672-74 Barrington Street (right)

Like Edward Elliot, Dumaresq chose the modern Chicago style. The building is constructed of grey brick with red brick and terra cotta accents. The feeling of height is achieved by the acceleration of detail towards the top of the structure — the arched windows and the high rooftop parapet. The window pairs are divided by costly red marble colonnettes which account for the nickname "marble building". The avant-garde office building attracted avant-garde tenants like Guglielmo Marconi who invented wireless telegraphy; he operated an experimental broadcasting station in the building for four years.

Not to be outdone by the Nova Scotia Furnishing Company, the rival firm of Gordon and Keith, eastern Canada's "oldest and largest" dealership in house furniture, carpets, pianos and organs, retained architect William Tuff Whiteway in the spring of 1896 to design the Keith Building. Whiteway was an experienced and well-travelled architect. A native of St. John's, Newfoundland, he had spent time in San Diego and practised in Vancouver in the late 1880's, designing buildings in the Gastown area.

In Halifax, he designed several houses including one on Young Avenue. But it was the substantial Keith Building which won acclaim; a handsome perspective drawing appeared in the March 1897 issue of *Canadian Architect and Builder*. Whiteway's design was influenced by the Chicago School with its series of high Romanesque arches, profusion of top-storey windows and wide frieze of recessed brickwork below the roofline. The surfaces are decorated with terra cotta panels and tall reeded sandstone pilasters. For several years after the completion of the Keith Building, Whiteway's own office was located there.

In 1906, the Chicago style influenced the design of the No. 6 Fire Hall. Though the city's new service structure did not exhibit extra height like the commercial buildings, the fenestration and ornamentation follow Chicago's lead. The tall pilasters, the wide Romanesque window arches beneath tripartite sets of narrow windows, all signal the style. On the Bedford Row elevation, the wide arches were once doors through which the horse-drawn fire engines rushed to meet emergencies!

It is somewhat ironic that the grand-scale architecture of the mid-western metropolis of Chicago influenced the small-scale buildings of the little seaport on Canada's east coast. Yet in Halifax, the Chicago style was a definite turning point. Halifax had finally begun to take on a North American appearance. The early Chicago style fitted admirably into the context of British and European styles, adding a new decorative dimension but harmonizing in scale and proportion. However, 20th century offspring, the monolithic high-rise towers, disrupt traditional building sizes and threaten the increasingly rare historic architecture with extinction □

Plate 55.   Old No. 6 Fire Hall, 1679 Bedford Row

Plate 54.   Keith Building, 1581-89 Barrington Street

PACIFIC BUILDING
1537-47
Barrington Street

FREEMASONS' HALL
1533 Barrington Street

This pair of early 20th century buildings are similar in scale and volume but exhibit their individuality in design and construction materials.

The construction material of the Pacific Building is rare in Halifax — white glazed terra cotta or ceramic blocks set in courses like stone. Built in 1911 for the Young Men's Christian Association, the building was designed by New York architects, Jackson and Rosencrans, who had designed Y.M.C.A. buildings in Ottawa, Winnipeg and Montreal. This building has a deeply recessed central section behind a long, low balustrade. Raised moulded panels and mock corner quoins along with recessed, decorated semi-circles all contribute texture to the smooth surface of the building.

About the same time, the Freemasons were also planning for a new building. In 1910 the adjacent corner lot was purchased for $17,100, but the First World War intervened before the project got underway. The cornerstone was eventually laid on May 2, 1924, by James H. Winfield, Grand Master. Winfield's executive and financial experience with the Maritime Telegraph and Telephone Company proved invaluable during the critical construction period.

The Freemasons' brotherhood has ancient roots in the medieval craftsmen's guilds. In Halifax, the first governor, Edward Cornwallis, himself an active Freemason, and four other founding fathers, William Steele, William Nesbitt, Robert Campbell and David Haldane, established the first lodge in 1750 while the pioneer settlement was still under construction. The earliest meeting places of the Grand Lodge included a room "over the Market House", the Golden Ball Tavern, and two subsequent wooden masonic "temples".

The present magnificent masonry structure marked a culmination for the long-standing benevolent society. Architect Sydney Perry Dumaresq created dramatic modern visual effects with traditional classical elements; eight sandstone pilasters span the brick upper storeys and tall arched windows dominate the linear panels between the pilasters. Instead of smaller top-storey windows on the front elevation, Dumaresq used five unusually elegant sandstone medallions symbolic of the elaborate ceremonial medallions of the masonic order. The uniquely decorated Freemasons' Hall and the uniquely constructed ceramic Pacific Building add a special dimension to the city's built heritage□

Plate 56.   Pacific Building, 1537-47 Barrington Street (left) and Freemasons' Hall, 1533 Barrington Street (right)

Saint Mary's congregation grew from humble beginnings and overcame punitive laws of persecution which forbade Roman Catholics from owning land, building churches and worshipping in public. In 1759, any person who harboured a "popish priest" would have been fined £50 and "set in a pillory". Five Irish Catholics of Halifax petitioned the Governor of Nova Scotia for the repeal of the laws, and finally on July 2, 1784, religious freedom was granted by King George III.

Seventeen days later, the small wooden frame of the first church, known as St. Peter's, was put up. By the spring of 1820, Bishop Edmund Burke had begun constructing a sturdy ironstone cathedral next to the old wooden church. The cathedral was called St. Peter's like its predecessor until 1833 when the wooden church was carefully dismantled and sent across the harbour, along with its rightful name, to become the first Roman Catholic church in Dartmouth. Thus the cathedral acquired the new name of St. Mary's.

In 1863 Archbishop Thomas Connolly initiated substantial changes to Edmund Burke's restrained Georgian Gothic cathedral. The building was lengthened and the interior was entirely reworked. But the most startling transformation was the addition of a grand Victorian facade fashioned in white granite. In 1868 when Archbishop Connolly requested permission from the Foreign Office in London to quarry the required seven hundred tons

of granite, he noted: "There is enough stone in that quarry to build all the fortifications of the British Empire and after to build as many cities as large as London."

Permission was given and the project undertaken according to the design of New York architect Patrick Charles Keely. An acknowledged authority, Keely had produced designs for approximately 500 North American churches. On September 7, 1874, the monumental facade was completed and the cross was placed 189 feet above ground, at the top of the highest dressed granite spire in North America.

In 1950, Pope Pius XII conferred the title of Basilica on the venerable church□

Plate 57. St. Mary's Basilica, Spring Garden Road, from the Old Burying Ground

By the late 19th and early 20th centuries, the downtown had become a sophisticated commercial centre. The high degree of sophistication was particularly evident in specialized corner buildings. The 'wrap-around' architectural treatment at corner locations not only provided a clever visual definition but took advantage of the extra commercial opportunities of shop frontage on two streets.

The Dillon Building at the corner of Sackville and Market streets is a beautifully articulated corner building combining a series of granite pilasters on the first storey and brick pilasters with granite capitals on the upper storeys; the cornice features paired brackets above each pilaster and a band of intricate brickwork. The Dillon Building features a rare diagonally sliced corner.

The Dillon Building was constructed sometime after 1879 when three brothers — John, William and Dennis Dillon acquired the property at a public auction and established a flourishing grocery store. From their new building, Dillon Brothers sold "choice coffees, canned goods, butter, cheese, ham, bacon" and a selection of "foreign and domestic green and dried fruits". They also advertised themselves as "vegetable contractors" promising prompt attention and free delivery!

The intersection of Barrington and Blowers streets is especially distinctive with two 'wrap-around'

structures on diagonally opposite corners. On the northwest corner stands the four-storey Farquhar Building. Constructed in 1897, the brick building housed the firm of James and Robert Farquhar. The brothers, James, a tinsmith, and Robert, a gas fitter, combined their talents in the plumbing, heating and electrical fields.

On the southeast corner of Barrington and Blowers is the smaller scale Brown Building. It was designed in 1910 by architect Richard Arthur Johnson for William M. Brown, a confectioner who lived and worked on the premises. Brown's Confectionery changed hands twice, becoming known as the Kandy Kastle in 1925. The characteristic rounded corner echoes the style of the Farquhar Building and creates a pleasing architectural balance at the intersection.

The tallest and most colourful corner building is situated at the southwest junction of Prince and Barrington streets. The yellow and red brick St. Paul's Building was constructed in 1897 for wealthy businessman, George Wright; the architect was James Charles Dumaresq, and Samuel Alexander Marshall was the builder. Tenants included the Belgian, Argentinian, Italian and Chilean consulates. Buckley Brothers was established in this building in 1897 by Dr. Avery Buckley. Since then, many generations have relied on Buckleys' Mixture cough syrup and Buckleys' White Rub for chest colds □

Plate 58. Dillon Building, 5268 Sackville Street

Plate 60. Brown Building, 1551 Barrington Street

Plate 59. Farquhar Building, 1558 Barrington Street

Plate 61. St. Paul's Building, 1684 Barrington Street

*A*lexander Hattie was the second son of John Hattie, a rugged and righteous Pictou County Scot. Like his father before him, Alexander had strong beliefs in God and in duty to mankind. He gave up his first career as a land surveyor to study medicine at the University of Pennsylvania. He also changed his name to McHattie, the rightful name of his pioneer ancestors.

Upon graduation, Dr. McHattie went to the Middle East as a medical missionary for the Presbyterian Church of the United States. While serving in Damascus, he wrote to a friend in Halifax about the alarming unrest in Syria. In one nearby town, Turkish soldiers had disarmed and sheltered more than one thousand Christians "for safety" and then allowed hostile Druses to slaughter them mercilessly. Two similar massacres followed in other towns, and the staff of the Presbyterian mission in Damascus lived in constant fear of attack. "God alone can avert it", wrote the faithful Dr. McHattie.

Finally the tension took its toll and Dr. McHattie's own health began to suffer. Still in his early thirties, he returned to Nova Scotia and set up a practice in the heart of downtown Halifax. He had the dignified brick townhouse with sandstone trim built in 1863; just below the bargeboards of the gabled dormers the letter "H" signified his ownership.

Dr. McHattie was one of the organizers of the Halifax Medical College, now the Dalhousie University Faculty of Medicine, and he himself lectured in Obstetrics. A finely-detailed portrait of Dr. McHattie, etched by his son, still hangs in the halls of learning as a tribute to his career.

In 1871, Dr. McHattie emigrated to Antigua where the warmer climate suited his delicate constitution. He sold his townhouse on Argyle Street to his partner, Dr. William B. Slayter, who resided there for many years □

Plate 62.   Dr. McHattie's House, 1706 Argyle Street

For more than a century this frame school house was the setting for innovative education. In 1818 the school was opened for both boys and girls who were "completely separated from each other" within the building. The school was successfully administered according to the Madras or National system which relied on only one schoolmaster and schoolmistress and numerous assistants or monitors. As many as 24 respectable gentlemen and 36 ladies, including the Countess of Dalhousie, helped with the instruction of the pupils. Since many of the children were from poor families, the Earl of Dalhousie, then Governor of Nova Scotia, provided stockings, mittens and coats for the young students one Christmas.

In 1902, the old National School became the first permanent home of the Victoria School of Art and Design, forerunner of the present Nova Scotia College of Art and Design. The school was the brainchild of Anna Leonowens, famed for her role as governess for the children of the King of Siam.

Years before, Anna Leonowens had begun her career as an educator after her husband's untimely death from sunstroke while hunting tigers near Singapore. At the age of 24, she opened a school for the children of military officers; her success was soon noticed by the Siamese Consul in Singapore and she was hired to teach the King's children for five years. Later she accompanied her daughter Avis to New York and opened a school on Staten Island. In 1876, when Avis'

husband accepted a managerial job with the Bank of Nova Scotia, Anna moved to Halifax with the family. In 1887, she began lecturing enthusiastically and circulating articles promoting the establishment of a school which would encourage fine arts and give "a higher artistic value to all the various branches of mechanical and industrial arts".

The idea was accepted and the Victoria School of Art and Design flourished in this building for 57 years□

Plate 63. The National School, 1744 Argyle Street

*T*he Presbyterian Church of Saint David was built in 1868 as the Grafton Street Methodist Church. The architect was David Stirling whose Italianate design for the Halifax Club had been widely acclaimed a few years earlier. The experienced contractor for the brick and sandstone structure was George Blaiklock.

Instead of designing a church with a steeple, Stirling created a Gothic Gable Church. The stunning composition was achieved by the wide angle of the great front gable, the tall Gothic buttresses and five fancy finials which project above the roofline. Preferred in smaller 19th century English towns, the Gable Church was thought to be a model of elegance and economy; the expense of a steeple was saved, but the abundance of miniature spires and elongated buttresses produced a dramatic Gothic church. This style was particularly suited to the Grafton Street Methodist congregation as Nova Scotia's first Methodist settlers came from Yorkshire, England, and were considered to be cultured yet thrifty folk.

In 1925, when the United Church of Canada was born by amalgamating Presbyterians, Methodists and Congregationalists, the Grafton Street congregation joined with St. Andrew's Presbyterian to form St. Andrew's United Church. The Grafton Street Church was then no longer needed by the Methodists.

However, members of nine Presbyterian churches in the Halifax area who did not wish to join the United Church formed a congregation and purchased the Grafton Street church for $30,000. This was an excellent price as the original cost of construction was $36,000!

Thus the small stone heads of John Wesley, the founder of Methodism, greet an equally cultured and thrifty Presbyterian congregation. The dual heritage of St. David's is especially satisfying in the modern ecumenical era□

Plate 64. St. David's Church, 1544 Grafton Street

Henry Busch was one of the city's most significant Victorian architects. He was born in Hamburg, Germany in 1826, and as a young man, travelled extensively in Europe. In 1847 he emigrated to Kentucky, but his health suffered from the sultry climate and he was advised to head north. He visited his uncle Walter in Chester, Nova Scotia, and by 1860 had married a sea-captain's daughter and settled in Halifax. In 1874 he officially became a Canadian citizen.

Undoubtedly Busch's European background influenced him to produce stylish, superbly decorative buildings. Because of the considerable regard for his talents, he was selected to design the Halifax Visiting Dispensary in 1875.

For the elevated, highly visible site at the south corner of Prince and Brunswick, he designed a striking brick building in the style popularized by the Emperor Napoleon III and the Empress Eugénie of France. Characteristically, the new medical clinic was given a mansard roof with tall chimneys and a partial cupola to accent the centre. A row of brackets trimmed the cornice and the rounded windows were grouped in pairs with one central triplet. The Dispensary cost $13,000 and housed a dental department, an apothecary's outlet, a clinic for eye and ear patients and even a coroner's office and morgue in the basement!

Three years later, Henry Busch was awarded the prestigious task of designing the Halifax Academy on the Sackville Street corner of the same block.

By 1878 Halifax had grown to 31,000 souls. Though a high school had existed since 1789, it had always operated in borrowed quarters. The decision to build proper premises for the institution occurred while the Rev. Dr. Edwin Gilpin was headmaster. Dr. Gilpin was a venerable figure in his "cassock and low-crowned hat", and he was a formidable disciplinarian; during his 41-year term the masters ruled with the leather strap.

In contrast to the severe dictates of the masters, Henry Busch designed a building of gracious elegance, at once complementing and embellishing the Second Empire theme of the nearby Dispensary. Looking even more like a French chateau, the Academy has a mansard roof with a full-blown, double-tiered cupola, and north and south projections to give the impression of attached pavilions or wings. Slim pilasters mark the visual "wings" and centre tower, while rounded windows appear separately in each wing and in stunning repeated triplets across the main facade.

When the Academy opened on January 9, 1879, Dr. Gilpin recorded the attendance of 68 distinguished guests, four masters and 79 boys. Girls were prohibited until 1885!

In that same year of enlightenment, the Salvation Army organized their first invasion of Halifax. On

Plate 65. Halifax Visiting Dispensary, 1697 Brunswick Street

Sunday evening of August 9, 1885, Captain Nellie Banks and her advance guard set out to "bombard the devil's kingdom"; they marched down the hill from Brunswick Street singing battle hymns, and preached from a wagon on the Grand Parade to 5,000 onlookers.

In 1892, when fire destroyed the Salvation Army hall on the north corner of Prince and Brunswick streets, Henry Busch was called upon to design the Army's new headquarters, the Salvation Army Citadel.

For his third building on Brunswick Street, Busch departed from the Second Empire style in order to create a military appearance for the "citadel" of the religious forces. Nevertheless, similar decorative elements maintain the visual connection with the earlier buildings. Vertical brick pilasters give the illusion of side towers, while horizontal bands of intricate brickwork decorate the centreline of the structure and complete the linear crest of each "tower". Dominant brick corbelling rises with a flourish to the apex of this fortress.

Henry Busch's trio of brick masterpieces on Brunswick Street are partners in the same setting; together they please the passerby and enhance the view from Citadel Hill □

Plate 66. Halifax Academy, 1649 Brunswick Street

Plate 67.   Salvation Army Citadel, 1707 Brunswick Street

*A*s Commander-in-Chief of the garrison, Prince Edward kept his finger on the pulse of every aspect of military life, from the construction of major new fortifications to the minutiae of the soldiers' daily routines. He readily admitted: "I never consider anything that happens within my command and that is connected with the King's service, as below my notice or attention."

He was an unyielding disciplinarian and ordered barbaric floggings for men who committed misdemeanors like drunkenness. He demanded perfect punctuality, though he was greatly hampered by the lack of a garrison clock. But like everything else he tackled, he remedied the situation on a grand scale. In 1798, during a sojourn in London, he ordered "a large clock" from the Royal clockmakers, the Swiss Vulliamy family.

The logistics of shipping the mammoth 1000-pound clock mechanism were handled by Sir Brook Watson who had spent some of his formative years in Halifax. Orphaned in England as a young boy, he was sent to work aboard the sailing ship of a distant Boston relative. One night while the ship was anchored in Havana Harbour he fell overboard and one leg was bitten off by a shark. While he was recuperating, his relative disappeared without a trace. Fortunately, a commissary agent from Nova Scotia heard of the boy's plight and brought him home to learn the business. Eventually, Brook Watson returned to England. He was appointed Commissary to the Duke of York's army in Flanders in 1793 and rose to the powerful position of Commissary-in-Chief of the British Army in 1798. In addition, he served as a member of Parliament and Lord Mayor of London.

By the spring of 1802, the total cost of manufacturing and shipping the clock, £351.16.5, was paid. By the following year, the heavy, hand-wrought iron clock frame with its myriad of brass cogs and wheels and 12-foot pendulum was installed in the suitably elegant baroque turret designed by William Fenwick (Plate 2). Sergeant Alexander Troop of the 29th Regiment, a Scottish-born watchmaker, set the works in motion.

The perfect precision of the parts and slowness of the movement are remarkable now, in an age when clocks run on a microchip and a battery. The Royal Clock has ticked away the minutes and hours for almost two centuries, and regardless of modern inventions, ticks on □

Plate 68. Royal Clock Mechanism, Old Town Clock, Citadel Hill

The most imposing structure inside the star-shaped walls of the great stone fortress is the Cavalier Building. Traditionally a "cavalier" is a high, two-storey military barrack building with a flat terreplein or gun platform on top. The Citadel's Cavalier originally fitted perfectly into the category. Designed by Colonel Gustavus Nicolls and built between 1830 and 1832, the Cavalier had seven 24-pounders mounted on its flat roof. Later, Lieutenant Colonel Patrick Calder's armament plan called for 32-pounder guns with an increased range of 3000 yards. About 1876, the gun-platform was permanently abandoned and the roof raised for extra barrack space.

Life for the troops in the barracks was rough and ready. Unlike today's armed forces who dine on nutritionally balanced meals with treats like cake and ice-cream for dessert, the mid-19th century soldier subsisted on monotonous basic rations — bread and tea for breakfast, boiled meat for dinner and tea and left-over bread for supper. Even potatoes were a luxury which could be obtained if a soldier's pay was docked a few extra pence per day. Between 1856 and 1863 a private received a salary of one shilling per day with an extra one penny for the purchase of beer. But the meager wage was quickly depleted with a charge of 4 1/2 pence per day for food and other charges or "stoppages" when pay was withheld for clothing and equipment. The only guaranteed remuneration was the penny per day for beer!

Discipline was rigid and punishment harsh. A guilty solider could be flogged with a "cat-o'-nine tails" until flogging was finally outlawed by the British Parliament in 1881. Those convicted could also be imprisoned in one of the six cells located at the north end of the Cavalier Building. Sentences were sometimes accompanied by branding — a drum major would tattoo the convict on the left side, two inches below the armpit, with the letters D for deserter or BC for bad character. Gunpowder or ink was then rubbed into the wound to make the letters indelible!

Plate 69. Cavalier Building, Halifax Citadel

Plate 70. Barrack Room, Cavalier Building, Halifax Citadel

After the War of 1812, the territories of Maine conquered by the military and naval forces from Halifax were returned to the United States, but the funds collected during the occupation were retained. From these funds the Governor of Nova Scotia, the Earl of Dalhousie, "set aside" £ 1,000 to establish a garrison library. In a dispatch dated December 16, 1817, his reasoning was clear: "It ought not to be forgotten that the large funds at our disposal were obtained by the military from this command, and I do think a small part may be appropriated as a tribute of acknowledgement to that branch."

The Earl of Dalhousie later reported that £500 had been spent "in England on books of value and character" while a further £100 went "in New York on light reading". The assortment was appreciated in 1828 by Captain William Moorsom of the 52nd Light Infantry who hailed the library as a break from the "absolute monotony of the routine" during his "protracted residence".

When the British occupation of the island of Corfu ended in 1864, the books from the Corfu Garrison Library were shipped to Halifax. This lucky acquisition of leisure books for the 19th century gentleman on topics like travel, horseback riding and biography, greatly expanded the collection, and may have contributed to the eventual need for a new building.

In 1885 an agreement was negotiated with Mr. James Shand. The premises of the garrison library on Upper Water Street were transferred to him for use as a Sailors' Home; in exchange, Shand agreed to erect a suitable library building in Royal Artillery Park.

Styled with quaint plainness in an era known for its ornate architecture, the library is deceptive in size; the T-shaped extension behind the "entrance house" contains a spacious reading room with book-lined walls, and a sunny tearoom with views across the lawn.

In 1902 the library was named for the Duke of Cambridge who had served as Commander-in-Chief of the British Army for almost 40 years. For the record, "His Royal Highness greatly appreciated the compliment."□

Plate 71. Cambridge Military Library, Royal Artillery Park

*T*he enigmatic Bollard House has piqued the curiosity of countless citizens. Why is the old house so misshapen? Many an otherwise polite passerby has peeped momentarily through the old panes to see if the answer lies within. But the streets tell the story.

In 1812, the expansion of Royal Artillery Park necessitated a jog in Queen Street. In 1835, Dresden Row was lengthened to Sackville Street leaving an odd trapezoidal lot in between. When the perfectly symmetrical Georgian house was extended north-ward, the curiosity piece was created.

The three Bollard sisters, Alice, Bertina and Winnifred, inherited the house from their shipwright father, Charles Bollard, and his wife Sarah, who had housed their family there since 1904. The spinster sisters, exasperated by decades of public attention, often chased enthusiastic artists away from the house.

The present owners, Joyce and Paul McCulloch, sympathize with those who are fascinated by the Bollard House. Years before purchasing the strange old structure, Joyce McCulloch had been so capti-vated by its appearance that she commissioned an artist to paint it.

Inside, the owners have revived an old-fashioned convention — a quiet second-floor sitting room. Also in keeping with tradition, they have painted rather than stripped the mouldings, mantel, wide floor-boards, and the primitive, squared spokes of the stair rail. From the upper landing, a sense of the unhurried lifestyle of bygone days is all pervasive, like the flood of natural light through the old window panes □

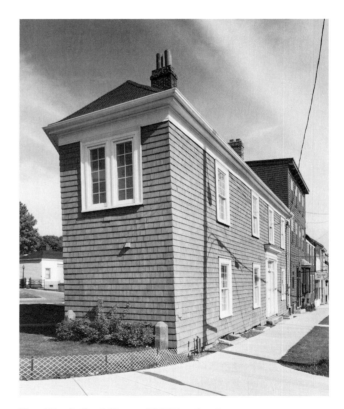

Plate 72. Bollard House, 1597 Dresden Row

Plate 73. Upper Hall Landing, Bollard House, 1597 Dresden Row

*I*n 1885 an American visitor described the Public Gardens as "a dream of beauty" and "the very perfection of landscape gardening". The overall design of the gardens had been created in 1872 by Superintendent Richard Power who had gained experience at Central Park in New York and the Duke of Devonshire's estate at Lismore, Ireland.

There are formal serpentine beds planted with colourful geraniums and natural floating beds where daffodils and tulips bloom in random profusion amid the grassy lawns. There are rose bowers and exotic trees like the Indian Bean Tree with large heart-shaped leaves, and the strange Oriental Plane Tree that sheds its bark annually rather than its leaves! In Griffin's Pond descendants of the royal swans donated by King George V glide regally about with dozens of bobbing ducks.

Man-made decorations delight the eye, too. Water cascades from fountains where cherubs ride leaping fish, and the central pathway is guarded by statues of three Roman goddesses — Flora, goddess of flowers, Diana, goddess of the forest and the moon, and Ceres, goddess of agriculture.

To commemorate Queen Victoria's Golden Jubilee in 1887, the gazebo or bandstand was added to the Gardens. Designed by Henry Frederick Busch, this fanciful architectural confection is the perfect centrepiece. And on a warm summer's evening, when the band is playing and dusk begins to fall on the magical world of the Gardens, it is easy to forget traffic and television and to be transported to a more leisurely era of hoop skirts and top hats, of musical soirées and strolls in the park □

Plate 74. The Gazebo, Public Gardens

Situated on Summer Street overlooking the lush foliage of the Public Gardens, the Garden Crest resembles an Edwardian resort with its tiered verandas and flamboyant roofscape.

The Garden Crest has the distinction of being the city's first luxury apartment house. When it opened in January of 1914 the *Morning Chronicle* described the layout and amenities. The most spacious suites, where the "privacy was just as complete as in the ordinary house", were arranged "in the college style with the parlours, diningroom, kitchen, pantry, etc. on one floor and the sleeping chambers on the floor above". Some suites even had separate maids' quarters, and there were three "dumb waiters" for carrying luggage and provisions to the units. The enthusiastic report also mentioned the white marble staircase with mahogany rails, and the ingenious "system of speaking tubes" for callers to communicate with the occupants.

Sidney C. Oland was among the first tenants. After acquiring the Highland Spring Brewery with his father in 1909, he joined the overseas war effort and led the long march from Mons to Cologne. Later he acted as aide-de-camp to three Governors-General of Canada and became one of Halifax's early preservationists. Colonel Oland advocated the retention of Keith's (Oland's) Brewery and Keith Hall, and he personally initiated the restoration of the Black-Binney House.

The Garden Crest was created for landowner George Wooten by a local architect, George Henry Jost in collaboration with the Montreal firm of J. J. LaFerme who had "much experience in this line of work". They used innovative fire-proofing techniques such as walls of asbestos plasterboard and concrete verandas.

From those verandas, many technological changes have been witnessed. Flying machines are light-years ahead of the ill-fated Hindenberg blimp that was an awesome sight as it floated above watchers at the Garden Crest in 1937. Today, highrise apartment towers share the neighbourhood with the Garden Crest, like oversized, plaster mannequins in the presence of a dowager queen □

Plate 75. Garden Crest Apartments, 1544 Summer Street

BAUER TERRACE

2083-2087
Bauer Street

TWELVE APOSTLES

2046-2068
Brunswick Street

auer's Field, owned by Thomas A. and John A. Bauer, was surveyed and divided into 54 building lots by June 12, 1855. Lots eight, nine and ten were soon filled with the attractive, Georgian-style cottage terrace known as Bauer Terrace. Though only one and a half storeys high, Bauer Terrace has many sophisticated features like mullioned sidelights, transoms, and distinctive Scottish dormers.

Bauer Terrace has been home to an interesting group of citizens. People like John Walsh, a rigger on sailing ships, and Alonzo Nickerson, a sea captain, lived at Bauer Terrace. Tinsmith Henry Schwartz and carriage-maker Alexander Hutt each occupied one unit when three Evans brothers — James, a stone-cutter, David a flour weigher and John a farmer — shared a unit.

The Twelve Apostles, originally named the Churchfield Barracks, were built in 1901 by the British Army. The neat terrace houses, with gabled dormers and shed porches ordered with military precision, were constructed according to English architectural plans. The barracks provided special accommodation for married soldiers.

The cozy housing units were a far cry from earlier living conditions. From the outset marriage was discouraged by the British Army. For years married couples were forced to live in ordinary barrack rooms "behind a makeshift divider of grey blankets and

sheets" for privacy. It was not until 1855 that the Army began to build special married quarters; even then, several families crowded into one barrack. The negative attitude towards marriage was especially focused on the ranks. In 1868, the number of married men was strictly controlled, and soldiers of less than 10 years service were not usually given permission to wed. The pitfalls of such a rash course of action were duly spelled out to perspective grooms in the Standing Orders for the Royal Artillery: "It is impossible to point out in too strong terms the general inconvenience that arises, and the evil consequences entailed upon individuals in a regiment encumbered with women. Poverty and the loss of independence is the lot of the married soldier." □

Plate 76. Bauer Terrace, 2083-2087 Bauer Street

Plate 77. The Twelve Apostles, 2046-2068 Brunswick Street

*T*he bulky, rock-faced baronial towers of the Armouries provide an imposing show of strength. Built between 1896 and 1899, the sturdy regimental drill hall proved to be a massive construction project.

The principal building material was the distinctive red sandstone from Pugwash. The unshakable foundation required 16,000 cubic feet of granite. Nine 40-ton, steam-driven derricks with 70-foot booms lifted loads of bricks and hoisted the finished stones into place. More than 60 labourers worked in gangs cutting stones, laying bricks and mixing the necessary 35,000 barrels of cement.

The contractor, J. E. Asquith, paid the brick-layers three dollars for a nine-hour day and the stone-cutters 30 cents an hour. Even with low wages, however, the total cost of construction amounted to more than $200,000.

On June 27, 1899, 500 militiamen of the 63rd Halifax Rifles and the Princess Louise Fusiliers marched from the old shed on Spring Garden Road to take over their new drill hall. And less than three months later, Britain became embroiled in the Boer War against the Dutch-speaking republics of Transvaal and the Orange Free State in southern Africa.

For the first time in Canada's history, companies of volunteer troops were raised for a foreign war. To the first contingent, Nova Scotia contributed H Company

with numerous men from the 63rd Halifax Rifles and the Princess Louise Fusiliers. On January 19, 1900, the Halifax citizenry hosted a grand farewell reception at the Armouries for 1,320 field artillery and cavalry men of the second contingent.

Before it had stood a year, the Armouries and its militia troops played a significant role in the Boer War and in Canada's emerging nationhood □

Plate 78. The Armouries, Cunard Street

On October 27, 1873, an article in the *Halifax Evening Reporter* commented on the astonishing rapidity of new residential development north of the Commons "where a short time ago, there was nothing to be seen but pasture or potato fields". By then, three of these stuccoed brick houses were finished and others were underway. The *Reporter* noted the "tightness of the money market" and marvelled at the entrepreneurial daring of Mr. Andrew Mooney, the builder and mason: "Mr. M. is a pushing, enterprising mechanic, and we hope his endeavours to improve and build up the northern suburbs of the city will meet with due encouragement."

Andrew Mooney's cul-de-sac development "for persons of moderate means" was highly successful. when he advertised the "very snug and comfortable" houses for sale, buyers soon purchased the commodious seven room dwellings all "fitted up with gas and water and finished in modern style".

Owners like Ambrose Allen, a sailmaker, David Whiston, a silversmith and watchmaker, Joseph Purdy, a sea captain, and Milledge Ruggles, who ran a glass and crockery firm, must have made an interesting neighbourhood.

In 1890 Andrew Mooney moved into one of the houses himself. By then he had built more houses along Cunard Street, was overseer of the new construction at the Victoria General Hospital and had served as an inspector of works for the Intercolonial Railway.

Unfortunately he did not enjoy his abode on Princess Place for long, for he died suddenly on June 28, 1890, "from the ill effects of a carbuncle on his neck".

But more than a century later, eight of Andrew Mooney's well-built houses, secluded from the traffic of the nearby major arteries, are still as "snug and comfortable" as ever □

Plate 79. Princess Place

One of the horrors of slavery in the United States was that families were often split apart; children were taken from their parents to serve as labourers on other plantations. For example, a young boy named Richard Preston experienced just such a painful separation when he was forced to leave his mother. However, he never gave up hope of being reunited with her.

During the War of 1812, the British captured Washington. While the British fleet was stationed in Chesapeake Bay several hundred black slaves — men, women and children — escaped from the nearby plantations and flocked to the warships hoping for a passage to freedom. Vice-Admiral Sir Alexander Cochrane complied, and the blacks were transported to Halifax. Some stayed in town, while others, including Richard Preston's mother, settled across the harbour in a rural community coincidentally named Preston.

Due to the upheaval of wartime, Richard Preston had also escaped the bonds of slavery, making his way from Virginia to Upper Canada. Eventually in 1816, he migrated to Halifax in search of his mother. Upon hearing of the community called Preston, he sought her out, and mother and son were at last together again.

Richard Preston was a young man of great fortitude and compassion. Along with Rev. Burton, an Englishman and Baptist preacher, he travelled throughout the province to help minister to the black communities.

In 1831, the Baptists sent Richard Preston to London to complete his education in theology and to raise money to build an African Baptist Church. While he was away, a congregation was officially formed and a piece of land that had belonged to St. George's Anglican Church was purchased for £66.

Richard Preston was ordained on May 19, 1832, and returned home with approximately £500 that the West London Baptist Association had helped him collect. The following February, the House of Assembly granted a further £25 for painting and finishing the pews in the newly-constructed church. Rev. Preston, who served for 30 years, and the succeeding pastors have maintained the pioneer church as a focal point in the black community.

Cornwallis Street Baptist Church fits unobtrusively into the streetscape, a quiet architectural statement about the basic beliefs in freedom, equality and generosity that first brought its people together □

Plate 80. Cornwallis Street Baptist Church, 5457 Cornwallis Street

Among the most valuable treasures of vernacular architecture are the Georgian cottages in the city's north suburbs. Unlike the Schmidtville cottages which are more "urban" in style, these three northern examples fit into the rural cottage tradition.

Akins' Cottage was built in the 1790's by shipwright Winkworth Norwood, and is the city's oldest dwelling. The stark simplicity of the steeply pitched roof, tall chimneys and narrow gabled dormers indicate a true relic from the outskirts of the rough-hewn, garrison town.

For 55 years the cottage was the home of Thomas Beamish Akins. Akins, a native of Liverpool, Nova Scotia, acquired the property a few years after he was admitted to the bar in 1831. Though his legal practice produced a good living, his interest in history was paramount. In 1857, he convinced the government of the day to make provision for valuable historical papers "to be examined, preserved and arranged"; his enthusiasm also convinced the government to charge him with the task. Thus Akins became the first Record Commissioner or Provincial Archivist in the British North American colonies. He held the post for 34 years, cataloguing 500 volumes of documents and personally amassing 3000 important books. When into his eighties, the tiny Dickensian gentleman with bright eyes and wispy white hair could be seen leaving Province House as the workday closed, wearing a short frock coat, a top hat and high collar wrapped about with a bulky neckcloth. At his cottage on Brunswick Street he always entertained his visitors with vivid and amusing anecdotes.

Farther north on Brunswick Street, Hope Cottage, which dates from the first decade of the 1800's, is in the "Cape Cod" style with a central doorway and two small windows on either side. But the mixture of construction materials, brick for the front and north exterior walls and wood cladding for the south wall, is individual. The gabled dormers and the low scale of the little residence produce an appealing antique charm.

On Gottingen Street, Bellevue Cottage is a little more decorative with attractive moulding and bracketed entablatures above the front windows. The hipped-roof dormers, fairly prevalent in Georgian times, are now a rare sign of age.

In 1821, Benjamin Etter, a watchmaker and jeweller, built himself a fine residential estate at the corner of Gottingen and North streets. This estate, known as Bellevue, was soon passed on to Etter's daughter, Mary Ann, and her husband, the Honourable William A. Black. Black and his brother had been apprenticed to Benjamin Etter before setting up their own business as jewellers and silversmiths. Although the Bellevue mansion no longer stands, the picturesque worker's cottage which housed successive gardeners and coachmen, is still a reminder of the bygone days of horse-drawn carriages and country living □

Plate 86. John Conrad West House, 2287 Brunswick Street

Plate 88. Parsonage & Townhouses, 2138 and 2140-2146 Brunswick Street

Plate 87. Nathaniel & William West House, 2319-2323 Brunswick Street

*I*nitially, when the Roman Catholic faith was outlawed, this congregation worshipped secretly in a barn located on the northwest corner of Gottingen and Gerrish streets. When religious freedom was granted in 1784, an unused Protestant meeting house on Brunswick Street was purchased. The same site was used for the present St. Patrick's Church.

On August 8, 1883, several thousand spectators watched as the cornerstone was laid by His Grace Archbishop Cornelius O'Brien. Inside the corner-stone, a tin box contained memorabilia like copies of the constitutions of the Charitable Irish Society and the Catholic Total Abstinence Societies as well as coins, newspapers and the autobiography of newly consecrated Archbishop O'Brien.

The 36-year old Archbishop's autobiography was interesting. Born in rural Prince Edward Island, he had left home at the age of 16 to seek his fortune in the business world. But he soon became disillu-sioned and entered St. Dunstan's College in Charlot-tetown. His extraordinary ability led the Bishop of Charlottetown to send him to Rome where he obtained his doctorate in Divinity. He returned to teach at St. Dunstan's but delicate health forced him to take up lighter duties in a rural parish. He was a shy, sensitive man, a poet with no love of public speaking and no administrative experience. His unexpected selection to lead the archdiocese was like calling a wild card, but proved to be the perfect move.

Henry Peters, who prepared the architectural plans for the pleasing brick and granite Gothic church, was an older man in the sunset years of his career. In fact, Peters had acted as a contractor more often than an architect, but in this case his design was preferred above those submitted by architects in New York and Boston. Peters had come to Halifax from Montreal in 1855 to work for the military and had stayed on, building many houses and buildings. He was a prominent Roman Catholic and reported to be one of the "largest owners of property in the city".

For about two years, Henry Peters "pushed briskly ahead" with construction, aided by many "manifesta-tions of faith and zeal"; labourers offered their work gratuitously and others "contributed largely from their means". Finally "the happy day was at hand" on December 27, 1885; the faithful parishioners knelt before their old altar "in a new and magnificent church" □

Plate 89.   St. Patrick's Church, 2267 Brunswick Street

*I*t may have been a good omen for the future career of an 18-year-old emigrant Scottish lad that the vessel transporting him to the New World in 1845 was named the *Brilliant*.

By 1863 Sandford Fleming, a thoroughly educated and skilled engineer, set out to find the best route for the proposed Intercolonial Railway which was to link Halifax with Quebec. Consequently, he moved his family to Halifax and purchased this five or six-year old house on Brunswick Street in 1866 from its original owner, Martin G. Black.

In 1871, after the Intercolonial Railway was in progress, the new Dominion Government commissioned Fleming as Chief Engineer for the Canadian Pacific Railway project. Fleming went on to establish standard time zones throughout the world and to serve as Chancellor of Queen's University. He was knighted in 1897.

The twin gabled sections of the house provide a vernacular or carpenter's interpretation of a Gothic mansion. The massive chimneys, narrow gabled dormer and the uncommon board and batten cladding all heighten the vertical thrust of the design □

Plate 90. Sir Sandford Fleming House, 2549-2553 Brunswick Street

*A*dmiralty House must be one of the few stone houses that was supposed to have been built of wood. The reason for the mix-up was largely due to the difficulty of communicating across oceans in the days of sailing ships.

In 1809, Admiral Sir John Borlase Warren proposed the construction of an admiral's house "with a foundation of stone and the upper part of wood". Four years later in 1813, John Plaw, a noted British architect and author who had emigrated to the New World, had produced plans and specifications for an elegant frame structure on a stone foundation. Admiral Warren called for tenders on Plaw's proposal and proceeded to send both the plans and the successful tender to the Lords of the Admiralty in London for approval.

Before a reply was forthcoming, however, Admiral Warren was transferred and his successors had begun to build a stone house! When Rear-Admiral Edward Griffith finally received the approved plans for a wooden house in July of 1815, "three-fourths of the basement storey was raised and every necessary preparation made for constructing a stone building".

Rear-Admiral Griffith overcame the dilemma by continuing to build a stone superstructure under the direction of chief mason John Rhind. The interior layout, however, bears a marked resemblance to the layout of the wooden admiral's house designed by John Plaw.

During World War I, Admiralty House served as a naval hospital; the elegant reception rooms became wards, while the kitchen was transformed into an operating theatre and the basement doubled as a temporary morgue.

Throughout the over-crowded, bustling years of World War II, Admiralty House had a happier role as the Officers' Mess for H.M.C.S. Stadacona. Hundreds of Canadian naval officers dined there; on average, 600 meals a day were served, with six or seven shifts for lunch alone.

Now a National Historic Site, Admiralty House functions as the Maritime Command Museum □

Plate 91. Admiralty House, C.F.B. Stadacona

FERNBANK

2730-2740 Gottingen

J. WESLEY SMITH
MEMORIAL
CHURCH

Robie Street
at Charles

*T*he turreted Second Empire manor called Fernbank was built in 1878 as the home of J. Wesley Smith, a wealthy "merchant prince". In the 1860's, he and his brother Edmund had founded the drygoods firm of Smith Brothers on Granville Street. Though the business began on a modest scale, J. Wesley Smith's "rare business aptitude and a persistency of purpose" soon led to great prosperity.

But Smith's life was not totally consumed with the world of commerce and finance. His strong Methodist upbringing in Windsor, Nova Scotia, greatly influenced his decisions. He declined bank directorships in favour of onerous educational and spiritual duties. He served on the public school-board and on the board of regents of Mount Allison University. As a member of Brunswick Street Methodist Church, he became involved in missionary work in the city's north suburbs. Eventually he left the Brunswick Street church and identified himself solely with the Charles Street Mission. The mission was "signalized by phenomenal success", and soon the cornerstone for a fine new church was officially laid by J. Wesley Smith in 1902.

Unfortunately he did not live long enough to see the edifice named in his honour, the J. Wesley Smith Memorial Church. The asymmetrical configuration of the Gothic church with five gables and an octagonal turret provide a varied plan. The prominent corner buttresses and broad Gothic windows in the gables

juxtaposed with the narrow window slits in the turret, create a medieval aura. The corner location of the church is accented by the diagonal placement of the main doorway and the remarkable narrow rectangular belfry reminiscent of the "clochers à peine" found in southern France. Above the gables, belfry and turret, the multifaceted roofscape is capped by a wide octagonal cupola.

The originality of the design, prepared by the architectural firm of Hopson Brothers, is not surprising. English-born and trained, Charles H. Hopson had a distinguished career as a leader of the firm and an educator. For many years he taught architecture at the Victoria School of Art and Design □

Plate 92. Fernbank, 2730-2740 Gottingen Street

Plate 93. J. Wesley Smith Memorial Church, Corner of Robie and Charles Streets

*J*ust after 9 a.m. on December 6, 1917, the munitions ship *Mont Blanc*, carrying 4,000 tons of T.N.T., collided with the Belgian relief ship *Imo* in Halifax harbour. In the resulting explosion, two square miles of the city's north end were blasted to smithereens in two seconds. The fire that broke out instantly in the wreckage was quenched to a state of smoldering ruins by the wintry blizzard that followed. More than 1,500 people were killed and thousands were left homeless.

Rescue and rebuilding were carried out with unprecedented dedication under the direction of the Relief Commission. At first, builders worked day and night to clear the rubble and put up temporary shelters on the Commons for about 5,000 people. Then, with donations amounting to millions of dollars, the most extensive permanent housing scheme in Canada was launched.

The centrepiece of the massive reconstruction was the hydrostone district. Thomas Adams, a town planner from Ottawa, and the Montreal architectural firm of Ross & Macdonald conceived a comprehensive plan for streets, green spaces, shops and houses. For example, eight streets were laid out with courts or broad boulevards 300 feet long by 140 feet wide. The 326 dwellings of the court development were predominantly attached terrace houses; the houses as well as the shops on the perimeter of the development were all designed as variations on the "picturesque Tudor cottage" style. The combinations of half-timbered stucco and hydrostone with gambrel, gable and hipped roofs created a neighbourhood of cohesive charm and variety.

The hydrostone building blocks were manufactured locally from a mixture of gravel, crushed stone, sand and Portland cement moulded together by heavy compressing machines exerting 150,000 pounds of pressure. The large 24 inch by 9 inch size of the blocks and an output of 4,000 blocks per day, meant that buildings could be rapidly constructed with relatively few masons.

Thus Halifax was rebuilt in the short span of two years. The pleasing nature of the hydrostone development probably softened some of the horrors of the tragedy. Now age allows a well-deserved heritage status to the district, a lasting and useful monument to human generosity, skill and courage in the face of disaster □

Plate 94. Young Streetscape, Hydrostone District

Halifax has always celebrated the presence of royalty with enthusiastic entertainment. In 1787, when Prince William's frigate *Pegasus* put into port at Halifax, citizens lit candles in their windows as a sign of welcome, and a grand ball was held in his honour. Seven years later, William's younger brother Edward arrived to command the garrison. The fact that Prince Edward had a beautiful French mistress heightened the excitement.

While stationed in Gibraltar, a few years earlier, Prince Edward had commissioned a confidant to find him a mistress to ease the boredom and frustration of his solitary life. Accordingly, Thérèse-Bernardine Mongenet, an experienced French woman who had served as mistress to two French noblemen, was engaged for the purpose. When Edward was transferred to Quebec, he adamantly refused to give her up. For the sake of propriety in the New World, she assumed the fictitious name of Madame de St. Laurent, a supposedly widowed noblewoman.

In spite of her more respectable status, the couple were snubbed socially in Quebec. In Halifax, however, they became the darlings of the town's social life, attending balls, levees and plays. After one gala performance at the theatre, the zealous audience broke into choruses of "Rule Britannia", and after another, the *Halifax Weekly Chronicle* published a glowing poetic ode, "On Seeing Mme St. L ——— dressed in DIAMONDS at the THEATRE".

Governor John Wentworth doted on the young prince and his paramour with a mixture of fatherly concern and deference. "It is highly necessary, in these democratic times, that every possible distinguishing respect should be paid to the Royal family," he wrote. And since there was no official residence for the commander of the garrison, Wentworth loaned the couple his own property on the Bedford Basin.

There Prince Edward and Julie, as she was known privately, created a romantic country estate with winding paths that spelled her name, a heart-shaped pond and ornamental Chinese and classical garden temples among the trees. One classical temple remains, the Rotunda, a stunning architectural jewel with its circular colonnade supporting the broad dome and large rooftop ball. Sometimes referred to as the music pavilion, the Rotunda was likely the setting for glittering musical soirées where the Prince's band played and Madame delighted the guests with her fine singing.

There was an ending to this idyllic life. Prince Edward eventually gave up his beloved mistress to father Queen Victoria. But maybe it would have pleased the Prince to know that half a century later, his Prince's Lodge grounds were the scene of a grand Civic Picnic in honour of another visiting prince, his grandson Prince Arthur. Maybe it would also please him to know that the Rotunda still reminds us of his lady and their love affair □

Plate 95. Prince's Lodge Rotunda, Rockingham

Arcade: series of arches

Balustrade: railing along the edge or top of a roof

Baroque: ornate classical style of architecture popular in the 17th and early 18th centuries

Bartizan: small turret-like projection usually found at corners

Bracket: ornamental support for roof cornice, arch, entablature

Buttress: supporting element against wall; often a purely decorative rather than structural member

Clerestory: upper section of church walls pierced by windows

Clocher à peine: comb-like belfry prevalent in France

Colonnade: row of columns supporting roof, veranda or entablature

Corinthian: type of classical decoration including icanthus leaves

Corbel: bracket

Cornice: projection between roof and top of exterior walls of a building

Coved: high ceiling curved to meet junction with wall

Crenellated: notched or loopholed top of wall

Cupola: rounded or polygonal dome crowning a structure

Dentils: small teeth-like blocks decorating base of cornice, entablature

Entablature: horizontal band topped with a moulded projection used above doors, classical columns, windows

Fanlight: fan-shaped (semi-circular or elliptical) window

Finial: linear, pointed ornament frequently found at apex of gable, pediment

Frieze: decorative band along top of wall

Frontispiece: projecting section of a structure

Gable: triangular top of an end wall or dormer or triangular line of the eaves of a roof

Gothic style: style of architecture with pointed arches prevalent in western Europe from the 12th to 16th centuries

Hip or Hipped-roof: roof with sloped ends as well as sides

Mansard roof: style invented by François Mansard in 17th century France; double sloped roof with steep curved lower slope; often "half-mansard" with double slope only on front of roof

Martello: generic term for coastal defence tower

Moulding: a continuous linear or lined ornament

Mullion: vertical strip dividing window panes

Oriel: a rounded or multi-sided projecting window

Parapet: a low wall along the edge of a roof

Pediment: triangular decoration used above doors, windows, porches or on the gable ends or fronts of buildings

Pilaster: an ornamental half-column projecting slightly from a wall

Queen Anne style: turreted, asymmetrical style of architecture popular from about 1880 to 1920

Quoins: decorative structural stones, short and long faces laid alternately

Romanesque style: style of architecture with rounded arches originating in Romanized Europe from the 10th century to Gothic period

Segmental: slightly curved arch forming an angle at each side

Transom: horizontal rectangular window above a door

Trefoil: three-lobed ornament

Trompe l'oeil: imitation which fools the eye

Truncated: sliced off or flat-topped

BIBLIOGRAPHY

Akins, Thomas Beamish, *History of Halifax City*, facsimile edition of the 1895 publication, Mika Publishing, Belleville, 1973.

A Century Ago, Halifax 1871, a facsimile edition of *Rogers' Photographic Advertising Album of 1871*, reprinted by Heritage Trust of Nova Scotia, Halifax, 1971.

A Sense of Place, Granville Street, Halifax, Nova Scotia, Heritage Trust of Nova Scotia, Halifax, 1970.

An Evaluation and Protection System for Heritage Resources in Halifax, Planning Department, City of Halifax, 1977.

Armstrong, Frederick H., "Hay, William", *Dictionary of Canadian Biography*, University of Toronto Press, Vol. XI, pp. 391-393.

Articles and Minutes for a Halifax Dispensary: *Morning Chronicle*, April 13 and 18, 1876, *Halifax Reporter*, April 18, 1876, *Halifax Citizen*, April 18, 1876, *Acadian Recorder*, April 19, 1876, Minutes of March 16 and 23, 1875, and May 1875.

Articles regarding City Club: *Halifax Reporter*, September 9, 1872, *Acadian Recorder*, March 17, 1881, *Morning Chronicle*, May 6, 1886, *The Critic*, March 13, 1891.

Bach, Ira J., and Roy Forrey, editors, *Chicago's Famous Buildings*, The University of Chicago Press, Chicago, 1980 edition.

Barker, D. M. and D. A. Sutherland, "Collins, Enos", *Dictionary of Canadian Biography*, Vol. X, pp. 188-190.

Beck, J. Murray, "Young, Sir William", *Dictionary of Canadian Biography*, University of Toronto Press, Toronto, Vol. XI, pp. 943-949.

Bell, Winthrop, *The Foreign Protestants and the Settlement Of Nova Scotia*, University of Toronto Press, Toronto, 1961.

Bennett, Jim, "Shades of Studley Past", *Dalhousie Alumni Magazine*, Dalhousie University, Halifax, Winter, 1988.

"Black-Binney House, Hollis Street, Halifax, N.S.", Staff Report for Historic Sites and Monuments Board of Canada, Environment Canada Parks.

Blakeley, Phyllis R., "Cunard, Sir Samuel", *Dictionary of Canadian Biography*, University of Toronto Press, Vol. IX, Toronto, pp. 172-184.

Blakeley, Phyllis R., and Diane M. Barker, "Forman, James",

Dictionary of Canadian Biography, University of Toronto Press, Toronto, Vol. X, pp. 292-293.

Blakeley, Phyllis, John Devlin, Pat Langmaid, Kay MacIntosh, Elizabeth Pacey, Maud Rosinski, Garry Shutlak, research data contributed voluntarily on behalf of the Heritage Trust of Nova Scotia and the Landmarks Commission to the Planning Department, City of Halifax, 1976.

Blakeley, Phyllis R., *Glimpses of Halifax 1867-1900*, Public Archives of Nova Scotia, Halifax, 1949.

Boddy, Trevor, "Regionalism, Nationalism and Modernism, The Ideology of Decoration in the work of John M. Lyle", *Trace*, Montreal, Vol.1, No. 1.

Bowsfield, Hartwell, "Maitland, Sir Peregrine", *Dictionary of Canadian Biography*, University of Toronto Press, Toronto, Vol. VIII.

Bray, R. et al., *Exterior Recording Training Manual, Canadian Inventory of Historic Buildings*, Parks Canada, Ottawa, 1979.

Brosseau, Mathilde, *Gothic Revival in Canadian Architecture*, Canadian Historic Sites No. 26, Parks Canada, Ottawa, 1980.

Brown, Wayde, research briefs prepared on various buildings, for the Heritage Division, City of Halifax.

Buggey, Susan, "Building in Mid-Nineteenth Century Halifax: The Case of George Lang", *Urban History Review*, Vol. 9, No. 2, 1980, p. 5-20.

Buggey, Susan, "Building Halifax 1841-1871", *Acadiensis*, Vol. 10, No. 1, 1980, pp. 90-112.

Buggey, Susan and Garry D. Shutlak, "Stirling, David", *Dictionary of Canadian Biography*, University of Toronto Press, Toronto, Vol. XI, pp. 856-857.

Burroughs, Peter, "Prevost, Sir George", *Dictionary of Canadian Biography*, University of Toronto Press, Toronto, Vol. V.

Cameron, Christina, and Janet Wright, *Second Empire Style in Canadian Architecture*, Canadian Historic Sites No. 24, Parks Canada, Ottawa, 1980.

Canadians in Khaki, The Herald Publishing Company, Montreal, 1900.

Clerk, Natalie, *Palladian Style in Canadian Architecture*, Parks Canada, Ottawa, 1984.

Collins, Louis W., *In Halifax Town*, Halifax, 1975.

"Corner Stone Ceremonies of the New City Hall", August 18, 1888, and typescript of addresses by Mayor O'Mullin and Honourable Mr. Fielding, the procession, contents of the sealed box.

Dalhousie University Libraries 1867-1970, report manuscript, Dalhousie University, Halifax.

Devlin, John E. R., "Hollis Street homes form group that marks a passing century", *Mail-Star*, June, 1977.

Dixon, Roger and Stefan Muthesius, *Victorian Architecture*, Oxford University Press, 1978.

Duffus, A. F., G. E. MacFarlane, E. A. Pacey, G. W. Rogers, *Thy Dwellings Fair*, Churches of Nova Scotia 1750-1830, Lancelot Press: Hantsport, N.S., 1982.

Einarson, Neil, "Thomas, William", *Dictionary of Canadian Biography*, University of Toronto Press, Toronto, Vol. VIII, pp. 872-878.

Fergusson, C. Bruce, "T. B. Akins: A Centennial Commemoration", Nova Scotia Historical Society, Halifax, February 1, 1957.

Founded Upon A Rock, Historic Buildings in Halifax and Vicinity Standing in 1967, Heritage Trust of Nova Scotia, Halifax, 1967.

Gibson, M. Allen, "St. David's Presbyterian Church", *Chronicle Herald*, October 29, 1955.

Gillen, Mollie, *The Prince and His Lady*, reprinted by Goodread Biographies, Halifax, 1985.

Goodeve, Colonel H. T., *A Brief History of the Cambridge Library*, published by the library, Halifax, June 1, 1982.

Graham, Rev. Hugh, "Sketch of Brook Watson", Nova Scotia Historical Society, Halifax, Vol. 2, p. 135.

1819 Granville Street, Halifax, Canada, Nova West Properties Inc., Halifax.

Guide Handbook 1984, *Halifax Defence Complex, Historical Background*, compiled and printed by Visitor Services, Halifax Defence Complex, Halifax, May, 1984.

Halifax and Its Business, published by G. A. White, printed by Nova Scotia Printing Company, Halifax, 1876.

"Halifax Views", *The Canadian Illustrated News*, Montreal, July 6, 1872.

Hancock, Glen, "Halifax's Century-Old City Club Closes Its Doors", *The Atlantic Advocate*, March 1984.

Hanington, J. B., *Every Popish Person*, Archdiocese of Halifax, Halifax, 1984.

Harvey, D. C., "Newspapers of Nova Scotia, 1840-1867", *Canadian Historical Review*, Vol. XXVI, 1945, pp. 279-301.

Hattie, Robert McConnell and Joseph Howe Kirk, *Hattie Family Memoirs*, Imperial Publishing Co. Ltd., Halifax, 1936.

Henry, William A., *Map of Bauer's Field, Surveyed and Divided*, June 12, 1855, Plan C17, Registry of Deeds, Halifax.

Hill, Rev. George W., "Nomenclature of the Streets of Halifax", Nova Scotia Historical Society, Halifax, Vol. 15, pp. 1-22.

Hinds, Barbara, "Pond a relic of royal romance", *Mail-Star*, June 7, 1973.

Hutchinson, Thomas, *Provincial Directory*, Vols. for 1863 and 1864-1865.

"Improvements in the Northern Suburbs", *Halifax Evening Reporter*, October 27, 1873.

Johnston, C. H., "Cornwallis Street Baptist Church History", c. 1970.

Kent, V. Glen, "Binney, Hibbert", *Dictionary of Canadian Biography*, University of Toronto Press, Vol. XI, pp. 73-76.

Kernaghan, Lois K., "Blackadar, Hugh William", *Dictionary of Canadian Biography*, University of Toronto Press, Vol. IX, pp. 54-55.

"Laying of the Corner Stone of the New St. Patrick's", *Morning Chronicle*, August 9, 1883.

Legge, Lois, "Cambridge Library ... At one time it was "a very important part of town life", *The Novascotian*, April, 1985.

Logan, Major J. W., *A History of The Halifax Grammar School, High School, and Academy from 1789 to 1894*, Nova Scotia Historical Society, Halifax, 1936.

Longley, Ronald S. and Reginal V. Harris, *A Short History of*

Freemasonry in Nova Scotia, 1738-1966, Grand Lodge of Nova Scotia, Halifax, 1966.

Lotz, Jim, "Soup, soap and salvation", *The Southender*, August 1985.

MacLean, Andrew D., *R. B. Bennett, Prime Minister of Canada*, Excelsior Publishing Company Ltd., Toronto, 1935.

MacMechan, Archibald, "A Gentleman Of The Old School, He Played Leading Part In Saving Story of Province", *The Halifax Herald*, December 31, 1932.

McAleer, J. Philip, "St. Paul's Halifax, Nova Scotia and St. Peter's, Vere Street, London, England", *Journal of Canadian Art History*, Vol. VII, No. 2, 1984, pp. 113-136.

McAleer, J. Philip, *A Pictorial History of the Basilica of St. Mary's, Halifax, Nova Scotia*, Tech-Press, Halifax, 1984.

McAleer, J. Philip, "St. Mary's (1820-1830) Halifax: An Early Example of the Use of Gothic Revival Forms in Canada", *Journal of the Society of Architectural Historians*, Vol. XLV, No. 2, 1986, pp. 134-147.

McAlpine, David, et al., *Halifax City Directory*, Vols. for 1869-1896, 1903-1907, 1940's and 1967.

McIlveen, Claire, "Historic Oakville has a Hart-y past", *Mail Star*, March 7, 1987.

Maitland, Leslie, *Neoclassical Architecture in Canada*, Parks Canada, Ottawa, 1984.

Martell, J. S., "The Press of the Maritime Provinces in the 1930's, *Canadian Historical Review*, Vol. XIX, 1938, pp. 22-49.

"Military Making Improvements", *Morning Chronicle*, April 26, 1901.

Morrison, James, *Wave to Whisper...British Military Communications in Halifax and the Empire, 1780-1880*, Parks Canada, No. 64, History and Archaeology series, Ottawa, 1982.

Morrison, John, "Halifax Proud to bear Armouries", *The Leader*, October 18, 1986.

News item on Keith Hall, *British Colonist*, September 3, 1863.

"New Apartment House For Halifax", *Morning Chronicle*, January 1, 1914.

Pacey, Elizabeth, *Georgian Halifax*, Lancelot Press, Hantsport, N.S., 1987.

Pacey, Elizabeth, *Halifax Citadel*, Nimbus Publishing Limited, Halifax, 1985.

Pacey, Elizabeth, with G. Rogers and A. Duffus, *More Stately Mansions, Churches of Nova Scotia 1830-1910*, Lancelot Press, Hantsport, N.S., 1983.

Pacey, Elizabeth, "Long history behind Elk's Club building in downtown Halifax", *Mail Star*, May 24, 1977.

Perry, Margaret L., "The Armory and the Common", *The Atlantic Advocate*, September 1984.

Peterson, Jeannie, "1029 South Park Street, A Case Study", report for the Heritage Unit, Department of Culture, Recreation and Fitness, January 31, 1986.

Pryke, K. G., "Keith, Alexander", *Dictionary of Canadian Biography*, Vol. X, pp. 395-396.

Rosinski, Maud, research reports on various buildings, prepared for the Heritage Division, City of Halifax.

Rosinski, Maud, research data on Schmidtville, Point Pleasant Lodge, People's Bank and McHattie House, April 28, 1988.

Rosinski, Maud, *The West House, Brunswick Street*, Heritage Trust of Nova Scotia with Dineen Construction Ltd., Halifax, 1973.

Ross, Julie, "House fine example of Georgian period", *Mail Star*, May 10, 1977.

Saunders, Ivan J., *A History of Martello Towers in the Defence of British North America, 1796-1871*, Canadian Historic Sites No. 15, Parks Canada, Ottawa, 1976.

Service, Alastair, *Edwardian Architecture*, Thames and Hudson Ltd., London, 1977.

"Six Brick Houses", *Morning Chronicle*, October 29, 1874.

Soucy, Donald and Harold Pearse, *The First Hundred Years: A History of the Nova Scotia College of Art and Design*, Nova Scotia College of Art and Design, Halifax, in press 1988.

"Sudden Death", *Morning Chronicle*, June 28, 1890.

Sutherland, David A., "Wier, Benjamin", *Dictionary of Canadian Biography*, University of Toronto Press, Vol. IX, pp. 338-340.

The Canadian Encyclopedia, 3 vols. Hurtig Publishing Ltd., 1985.

"The City Hall, The Noble Structure Proposed", *Morning Chronicle*, October 21, 1886.

"The Opening of The New St. Patrick's Church", *The Evening Mail*, March 8, 1886.

"The Presbyterian Church of Saint David, Historical Sketch", information sheet published by St. David's Church, Halifax.

Tuck, Robert C., *Gothic Dreams*, Dundurn Press Ltd., Toronto, 1978.

Uniacke, Crofton, letter to his wife, Dorothy, September 17, 1807, PANS, MGl, Vol. 1769, No. 6.

"Valuable Real Estate For Sale", *The Novascotian*, April 26, 1838.

"Wanted - a Suitable Building for The Bank of Nova Scotia", published by The Bank of Nova Scotia, 1986.

Watkins, Ernest, *R. B. Bennett, A Biography*, Kingswood House, Toronto, 1963.

Watts, Heather, *On the Road from Freshwater Bridge, A History of the House at 5500 Inglis Street, Halifax, Nova Scotia*, Universalist Unitarian Church of Halifax, 1978.

Weir, Jean B., *The Lost Craft of Ornamental Architecture, Canadian Architectural Drawings, 1850-1930*, exhibition catalogue for Dalhousie Art Gallery, Dalhousie University, Halifax, 1983.

Wetmore, E. G. L., "New Play Therapy Room Honors Late Dr. Carney", *Mail-Star*, May 13, 1954.

Whitelaw, Marjory, *First Impressions, Early Printing in Nova Scotia*, Nova Scotia Museum, Halifax, 1987.

Whitfield, Carol M., *Tommy Atkins: The British Soldier in Canada, 1759-1870*, History and Archeology No. 56, Parks Canada, Ottawa, 1981.

Wright, Janet, *Architecture of the Picturesque in Canada*, Parks Canada, Ottawa, 1984.